1914–18 in Poetry

D1287841

1914-18 in Poetry

An anthology selected and edited by
E. L. BLACK M.A. M.Ed.

*Principal, Middleton St George
College of Education, Co Durham*

HODDER AND STOUGHTON
LONDON SYDNEY AUCKLAND TORONTO

ISBN 0 340 12421 0

Ninth impression 1986
Copyright 1970 E. L. Black

Printed in Great Britain for
Hodder and Stoughton Educational,
a division of Hodder and Stoughton Ltd,
Mill Road, Dunton Green, Sevenoaks, Kent,
by Page Bros (Norwich) Ltd

Preface

This anthology is intended for the upper forms of schools and for students in colleges of education. Among students in both schools and colleges there is a growing interest in the poetry of the First World War, partly as an illuminating source of information about a war that is just remote enough to interest many readers in a new way, and partly as an indirect comment on the political and ethical problem of our own age, which is so self-conscious about its interest in violence.

I have included poetry written *about* the First World War, whether it was written during the war or much later, and whether it was written by soldiers or civilians. Rather than arrange poems in chronological order of composition or in alphabetical list of authors, it seemed better to group it under sections.

Section 1 includes the poems that greeted the outbreak of war with an excited religious welcome as though it were a crusade: most of these poems were written by young upper-class recruits, but some were written by ageing civilians and some by regular soldiers.

Section 2 includes the poems in which individual poets first began to show awareness of the ghastlier side of war; these tended to be written at different times during the war because some poets got to the front line earlier than others. Owen in early 1917 and Sassoon in early 1916 had reached the stage in development of their personal ideas about war that Sorley had reached in early 1915.

Section 3 includes the poems whose main aim is realism; their writers are resolved to show civilians at home in 1914–18, and readers in future years, what the First World War was really like.

Section 4 includes the poems, notably those by Wilfred Owen, that stress the tragedy and waste of each soldier's death.

Section 5 includes the satirical protest poems that stress the stupidity of war, more than the tragedy of it, and try to expose the blunders of all who made it costlier than it need have been.

Section 6 includes the poems that manage to regard the war with a certain amount of detachment, whether it is old Thomas Hardy writing in 1917 from a Dorset village remote in place, or Ted Hughes writing in the 1960s from a point of view remote in time.

Some editorial comment is included. This is to help the modern reader when poets take for granted considerable knowledge of military details such as 'whizz-bangs' or '5·9s'. It is also to encourage the modern reader to admire the excellent poetry written about the First World War in defiance of critics who have undervalued it—notably Professor John H. Johnston in his critical study, *The English Poetry of the First World War*.

E. L. *Black*

Acknowledgments

Thanks are due to the following authors (or their agents or trustees) and publishers for permission to reprint poems, or to quote from the books listed: Richard Aldington, 'Bombardment' (Madame Catherine Guillaume); Herbert Asquith, 'The Volunteer' (Sidgwick & Jackson); Laurence Binyon, 'For the Fallen', 'The Sower', 'The Ebb of War' (The Society of Authors); Edmund Blunden, *Undertones of War* (A. D. Peters); G. K. Chesterton, *Collected Poems* (Miss D. E. Collins, Methuen and A. P. Watt); Clifford Dyment, *Poems 1935–48* (Dent); Wilfrid Wilson Gibson, *Collected Poems 1905–1925* (Mr Michael Gibson and Macmillan); Robert Graves, 'Dead Foxhunter', 'The Leveller', 'Two Fusiliers' (A. P. Watt); Ivor Gurney, 'To His Love' (Mr Ronald Gurney); Thomas Hardy, *Collected Poems* (The Trustees of the Hardy Estate and Macmillan); Sir Alan Herbert, 'Beaucourt Revisited' and 'After the Battle' (Methuen and A. P. Watt); A. E. Housman, *Collected Poems* (Cape and The Society of Authors); Ted Hughes, 'Bayonet Charge', 'Six Young Men' (Faber); Rudyard Kipling, *The Years Between* (Mrs George Bambridge, Methuen and A. P. Watt); Robert Nichols, *Ardours and Endurances* (Chatto & Windus); Wilfred Owen, *Collected Poems* (Mr Harold Owen and Chatto & Windus); Edward Vance Palmer, 'The Farmer Remembers the Somme' (Angus & Robertson); Max Plowman, 'Going into the Line' (Blackwell & Mott); Sir Herbert Read, *Collected Poems* (Faber); Ernest Percival Rhys, 'Lost in France' (Dent); Edgell Rickword, 'Winter Warfare' (Sidgwick & Jackson); Isaac Rosenberg, *Collected Poems* (the Author's Literary Estate and Chatto & Windus); Siegfried Sassoon, *Collected Poems* (Mr George Sassoon); Robert William Service, *Rhymes of a Redcross Man* (Benn); Sir Osbert Sitwell, 'Arm Chair', 'Judas and the Profiteer' (David Higham).

The cover illustration (Canadian infantry fixing bayonets before a charge on the Somme) is reproduced by courtesy of the Imperial War Museum.

Contents

4   The Pity of It

5   Bitter Satire

6 Comments from Remoter Points in Place and Time

In the first year or two of the 1914–18 war, poets such as Rupert
Brooke wrote enthusiastic poetry welcoming the war. Brooke himself
announced with eloquent over-confidence :

Now, God be thanked who has matched us with His hour.

The young soldiers who wrote poetry in these early months welcomed
the chance to live dangerously, and their poetry expressed an excited
disregard for their own personal safety.

Their slim volumes of verse became popular immediately and rapidly
achieved sales that very few poets have equalled since. Indeed, they
proved remarkably successful as amateur recruiting sergeants; their
poetry helped to urge the best of Britain's youth to volunteer in larger
numbers than the army could equip. For both good and bad reasons
their poetry retained its popularity with a comparatively wide public
throughout the First World War, and has never completely lost it.

Their techniques were like those of Britain's army in 1914—out-of-
date. But just as the British army of 1914–15, despite its unintelligent
generals and inadequate weapons, made a decisive contribution to final
victory, so the poets of 1914 and 1915 deserve a place of their own in
the halls of fame. Although their views on war were unrealistic and
their poetic techniques inadequate, their poems remain remarkable for
their sincerity and originality. Whatever the limitations of Brooke's
'The Soldier' and Julian Grenfell's 'Into Battle', they were quite
different from anything that had been written about war by most
previous poets. In English literature the only previous poets whose
writing about war could be considered much better than theirs
were Shakespeare and Byron, and perhaps Montrose, Hardy and
Kipling.

Brooke had not been dead long, however, before the more clear-
sighted of his fellow-poets saw the limitations of the poetry that he
typifies. Charles Sorley expressed in a letter his conviction that
Brooke's sonnets had been overpraised :

He is far too obsessed with his own sacrifice, regarding the going to
war of himself (and others) as a highly intense, remarkable and

sacrificial exploit, whereas it is merely the conduct demanded of him (and others) by the turn of circumstances.

Arthur Graeme West, who was killed in 1917, expressed his contempt of poets who wrote lines such as 'O happy to have lived these epic days' and ignored the revolting appearance of the dead and dying in actual warfare. One of his poems began with a direct attack on Brooke and his imitators:

God! how I hate you, you young cheerful men,
Whose pious poetry blossoms on your graves
As soon as you are in them.

But the latter half of the war produced a second generation of young soldiers, who produced very different kinds of war poetry from that of Brooke or Grenfell or Nichols. With blistering realism they portrayed modern war as it really is; sometimes, as in Blunden's descriptive poems, they stressed its unnaturalness; sometimes, as in Owen's most typical poetry, they invoked pity for the dead of both sides; sometimes, as in the satirical poems of Sassoon (and of the more intelligent civilians at home) they condemned all the generals, politicians, priests and profiteers who had failed to realize what a tragedy for humanity it was. These poets, especially Owen, have appealed to a smaller public than Brooke did, but they have retained a degree of popularity throughout the fifty years that have elapsed since Owen's death. Not only has their literary reputation grown steadily in the eyes of critics and scholars; also, the 1960s have increased their popularity with the common reader. There are two reasons for this: firstly, in 1964 the fiftieth anniversary of the outbreak of war in 1914 triggered off a series of books, television programmes and stage shows that made the First World War a fashionable topic; secondly, the war in Vietnam seemed to repeat some of the features of the earlier war, such as its lack of military movement, its static horrors for the private soldier, and the Pope's attempt to achieve a compromise peace.

Nevertheless, there has been an important minority of critics who have found in the second generation of war poets faults as serious as those in Brooke. In 1936, when W. B. Yeats compiled his anthology, the *Oxford Book of Modern Verse*, he excluded Owen's poetry, and defended this decision (in his introduction) on the grounds that 'passive suffering is not a theme for poetry'. When this exclusion of Owen's poetry was condemned by critics, Yeats defended his action in a bad-tempered letter to Lady Dorothy Wellesley:

When I excluded Wilfred Owen, who I consider unworthy of the poets' corner of a country newspaper, I did not know I was excluding a revered sandwich-board man of the revolution and that somebody has put his worst and most famous poem in a glass-case in the British Museum—however if I had known it I would have excluded him just the same. He is all blood, dirt and sucked sugar stick (look at the selection in Faber's Anthology—he calls poets 'bards', a girl a 'maid' and talks about 'Titanic wars').

Professor John H. Johnston of the University of West Virginia has written an interesting but ungenerous book *The English Poetry of the First World War*. His attitude to Owen's poetry is less cantankerous than Yeats's, but he argues that even the best poets of the First World War were too obsessed with the demoralization of modern war and were too close to their experiences to attain the heights of true tragedy. Repeatedly he criticizes the First World War poets for writing nothing longer or more complex than mere lyrics, which he insists are an inadequate medium for dealing with the 'vastly multiplied moral and physical confusions of technological warfare'. He accuses the war poets of limiting their subject-matter to 'disillusionment, anger or pity', and slates them for lacking comprehensiveness, objectivity and restraint. He argues that 'neither pity nor self-pity in themselves can inspire great poetry'. He protests even more loudly against the negative nature of Sassoon's satiric message and his inability to give the world any positive advice.

Johnston's arguments are unfair. These young poets, many of whom died in action, did not live long enough to write epics; all they could do was to scribble lyrics while cowering in shell-holes or enjoying their brief periods of leave. Owen, Sassoon and their fellow-poets wanted to show what war was like in the age of Haig, not the age of Achilles. In doing this they managed to achieve a wide variety of effects within the scope of the lyric. Certainly, they wrote much better poetry than the combatants in any other war, before or since; and as the first poets to tackle the subject of modern technological war, with its soul-shattering spiritual effects, they instinctively carried through a decisive revolution in literary technique. Possibly these poets were handicapped by not having inherited from the Georgian poets of 1900–14 flexible techniques that could deal effectively with the realities of modern war, but they showed inventiveness in improvising new techniques of their own. It is not true that their poetry is merely a presentation of passive suffering. For instance, although Wilfred

Owen's poem 'Dulce et Decorum est' may present the gassed soldier as dying in inglorious agony, the poem is a passionate appeal by Owen to humanity to face the truth about war, and the reader is intended to be aware of Owen and of humanity as well as the dying soldier. The impression that one gets of Owen's personality as one reads his poem is not that he is passive or helpless, for Owen and Rosenberg, even if their poems were not going to be published at once, felt that they had to bring home to civilians and others remote from the front line how terrible were the endurances and sacrifices of the fighting soldier. Similarly, Rosenberg's 'Dead Men's Dump' may depict 'the pitiable degradation of the slain', as Johnston puts it, but it does not give the impression that Rosenberg is pitiable or degraded—far from it.

Most of the readers who are moved by the poetry of Owen and Rosenberg are impressed by it at a first reading before they learn the facts of the writers' deaths. Even if these poets can be accused of writing about nothing except war, this is not a devastating criticism; it could be levelled just as easily at Homer or Virgil. Dr Johnson's lines about Charles XII of Sweden, Byron's stanzas on Waterloo, and Arnold's 'Sohrab and Rustum' are none the worse because they are about nothing but war. Until and unless atomic war destroys mankind, man's thoughts about war, especially its prevention, must remain of prime importance to humanity, and so poetry about it must remain of considerable importance too.

1914–18 in Poetry

1 Early Visions

In 1914 Europe blundered into the First World War. From 1870 to 1914 the Germans had built up a military machine of alarming efficiency. They seemed so certain of winning any war they entered that they became more and more proud of their wonderful army and more and more tempted to use it. Their successes in industry, in science and in the arts made them feel so arrogant and superior that they habitually tried to get their own way by threats.

This mood precipitated a series of international crises in each of which Germany reluctantly drew back from the cliff-edge of Armageddon. There followed the assassination in July 1914 of an Austrian archduke at Sarajevo by a Slav fanatic who thought that the Croats and other Slav races in Bosnia and Herzogovenia (now the northern part of Yugoslavia) should be allowed to join the Serbs, and should not be compelled to accept the foreign rule of the Austrians. The Austrian emperor and foreign minister continued to make unreasonable demands of the Serbs, whom they accused of encouraging the assassination. The German emperor and government irresponsibly allowed the Austrians to go further and further, though Germany, as the senior partner in the alliance, had the power to restrain Austria if she chose to. The Germans did not exactly *plan* to go to war in 1914, because they had no real plan. But they encouraged Austria to begin a local war with Serbia, despite the danger that it would rapidly produce a world war because Russia had promised to come to the aid of Serbia. A few days later the Germans made it impossible for France to break her promises to Russia, even if she wanted to, by demanding that France should hand over her key fortresses to Germany while Germany was fighting Russia. Germany also made it impossible for Britain to break her *vague* promises to France—by invading Belgium, to whom Britain had made *precise* promises. In short, the Germans' resolve to bully the world in 1914 was in its essentials similar to Hitler's in 1938 and 1939, though Hitler's policy was more melodramatic in detail.

It is difficult to see how Britain could have prevented the First World War or could have avoided taking part in it. The Germans were so powerful and so fond of bullying their neighbours that Britain could not have deterred them from beginning a world war. The German generals underestimated the British army so much that they took no notice of Britain's foreign minister. The tragic errors for which successive British governments can be blamed are not the failure to prevent war but the failure to conduct it efficiently. They promoted incompetent generals to command Britain's armies; they failed to supply their armies with enough modern weapons; and they allowed their generals to lose hundreds of thousands of lives in futile attacks on the Western Front, at a time in the history of warfare when science had given every advantage to the defender. Just as they had tried to fight the Crimean War with the methods and weapons of 1815, so they tried to fight the Germans in 1914 with the methods and weapons that had sufficed against the Dervishes.

Since it is difficult today to see how Britain could have avoided going to war in 1914, we must accept as still valid the reasons that some poets put forward in 1914 to justify Britain's entry into the war. In 1914 Thomas Hardy's poem 'Men Who March Away' claimed that

> braggarts must
> Surely bite the dust.

Kipling, similarly, insisted that

> The Hun is at the gate . . .

He urged the men of England to fight against a regime that acknowledged 'no law except the sword'; and he soberly warned them that

> No easy hope or lies
> Shall bring us to our goal.

Such poems may seem a little old-fashioned and self-righteous in their phraseology, but they express a point of view about the war that historians must still support. Britain had no real alternative but to fight in 1914.

Nevertheless, there are aspects of the British people's attitude to war in 1914 that were unrealistic, over-optimistic and sentimental; and much of the poetry written in the early part of the war, whether by young recruits or by elderly civilians, reflects these unrealistic attitudes.

The delusions of the Austrian and German peoples, most of whom welcomed the war, were shared, up to a point, by the British and by the other peoples whom the Germans compelled to fight. Each nation expected its army (and possibly its fleet also) to win an immediate decisive victory, as Prussia had won in 1870 and as Hitler was to win in France in 1940. Each expected to fight for a few weeks and then to dictate peace in the capital of its defeated enemy. No one expected a long war; no one foresaw that the war would be dominated by the stalemate of a static war in the trenches, and would end in revolutions and other gigantic social upheavals. Two examples of this lack of foresight will suffice: on 3 August 1914, Grey, then England's Foreign Secretary, said,

> If we are engaged in war, we shall suffer but little more than we shall suffer if we stand aside.

At the same time the German Army was deciding not to invade Holland because it expected to be allowed to trade freely with the rest of the world via Dutch ports.

The poets not only shared this general belief in a swift victory; they also believed that the war was a Christian crusade which would bring a new nobility to those who took part in it. Young men enlisted in a mood of optimistic exhilaration, assuming that the war would be both chivalrous and short, and would make them better people.

The poetry that some of them wrote expressed this mood. Its underlying assumption was expressed by John Lane, of the Bodley Head, who published in 1914 an anthology, *Songs and Sonnets for England in War Time*; his preface asserted:

> What can so nobly uplift the hearts of a people facing war with its unspeakable agony as music and poetry? The sound of martial music steels men's hearts before battle. The sound of martial words inspires human souls to do and to endure. God, His Poetry, and His Music are the Holy Trinity of War.

Even Siegfried Sassoon shared this view in his early poetry. In 'Absolution' he wrote:

> . . . war has made us wise,
> And, fighting for our freedom, we are free . . .
> We are the happy legion, for we know
> Time's but a golden wind that shakes the grass. ·

He wrote with joyful pride about his brother's death in Gallipoli and proclaimed that for him and his dead brother joining the army had

> made an end of all things base.

With unintended irony he wrote in his early poem 'France' :

And they are fortunate, who fight.

Similarly, Brooke thought of the soldier dying 'with all evil shed away' and insisted that in war

Nobleness walks in our ways again.

The brilliant young men of 1914 were in a hurry to die, like their spokesman Rupert Brooke who was in such a hurry to tell the world what would happen 'If I should die'. They did not regard the war as a wasteful tragedy that would rob them of a chance to use their talents constructively; they felt honoured to be chosen for the sacrifice.

In Brooke's sonnets 'To the Dead' he is proud and triumphant that they have

poured out the red
Sweet wine of youth.

He never feels any sense of waste that so great a sacrifice should achieve so little. He never stops to explain why, if Death achieves 'a white unbroken glory', it has to be death in war that does this.

In important ways the techniques that the poets of 1914 had inherited left them poorly equipped for writing poetry about modern war. The orthodox poetry of the time belonged to the type that the influential editor, Edward Marsh, included in his first volume of *Georgian Poetry* in 1912 and in the four volumes that followed. It lacked contact with science and industry, its emotions were gentlemanly and restrained; it enthused about the trivial details of rural life. Its vocabulary was artificially romantic and its metre was tediously orthodox. It lacked the vigour and the social purpose that was being shown in contemporary *prose* by writers such as Conrad, George Bernard Shaw and D. H. Lawrence.

There were, of course, important innovators waiting in the wings, but they had not yet had a chance to take the stage. Synge had urged poets to avoid the ornate diction of the late romantics, since

Before verse can be human again it must learn to be brutal.

W. B. Yeats, in his poems about Parnell and Irish politics, had begun to write with more colloquial force. Also the Imagists, such as T. E. Hulme, were resolved to introduce more vivid contemporary word-pictures and more flexible rhythm into poetry. But these innovations in poetry were at the same stage as many innovations in military science, such as the aeroplane; they had not had time to develop very far when 1914 created the need for their use on a much greater scale. In Britain the poets and soldiers of 1914 began the war with equally out-of-date techniques.

THE TRUMPET

Rise up, rise up,
And, as the trumpet blowing
Chases the dreams of men,
As the dawn glowing
The stars that left unlit
The land and water,
Rise up and scatter
The dew that covers
The print of last night's lovers –
Scatter it, scatter it !

While you are listening
To the clear horn,
Forget, men, everything
On this earth new-born,
Except that it is lovelier
Than any mysteries.
Open your eyes to the air
That has washed the eyes of the stars
Through all the dewy night :
Up with the light,
To the old wars;
Arise, arise !

Edward Thomas

MEN WHO MARCH AWAY
(Song of the Soldiers: 5 September 1914)

What of the faith and fire within us
   Men who march away
   Ere the barn-cocks say
   Night is growing grey,
Leaving all that here can win us;
What of the faith and fire within us
   Men who march away?

Is it a purblind prank, O think you,
   Friend with the musing eye,
   Who watch us stepping by
   With doubt and dolorous sigh?
Can much pondering so hoodwink you!
Is it a purblind prank, O think you,
   Friend with the musing eye?

Nay. We well see what we are doing,
   Though some may not see –
   Dalliers as they be –
   England's need are we;
Her distress would leave us rueing:
Nay. We well see what we are doing,
   Though some may not see!

In our heart of hearts believing
   Victory crowns the just,
   And that braggarts must
   Surely bite the dust,
Press we to the field ungrieving,
In our heart of hearts believing
   Victory crowns the just.

Hence the faith and fire within us
   Men who march away
   Ere the barn-cocks say
   Night is growing grey,
Leaving all that here can win us;
Hence the faith and fire within us
   Men who march away.   *Thomas Hardy*

INTO BATTLE

The naked earth is warm with Spring,
 And with green grass and bursting trees
Leans to the sun's gaze glorying,
 And quivers in the sunny breeze;
And life is colour and warmth and light,
 And a striving evermore for these;
And he is dead who will not fight;
 And who dies fighting has increase.

The fighting man shall from the sun
 Take warmth, and life from the glowing earth;
Speed with the light-foot winds to run,
 And with the trees to newer birth;
And find, when fighting shall be done,
 Great rest, and fullness after dearth.

All the bright company of Heaven
 Hold him in their high comradeship,
The Dog-Star, and the Sisters Seven,
 Orion's Belt and sworded hip.

The woodland trees that stand together,
 They stand to him each one a friend;
They gently speak in the windy weather;
 They guide to valley and ridge's end.

The kestrel hovering by day,
 And the little owls that call by night,
Bid him be swift and keen as they,
 As keen of ear, as swift of sight.

The blackbird sings to him, 'Brother, brother,
 If this be the last song you shall sing,
Sing well, for you may not sing another;
 Brother, sing'.

In dreary doubtful, waiting hours,
 Before the brazen frenzy starts,
The horses show him nobler powers;
 O patient eyes, courageous hearts !

And when the burning moment breaks,
    And all things else are out of mind,
And only joy of battle takes
    Him by the throat, and makes him blind,

Through joy and blindness he shall know,
    Not caring much to know, that still
Nor lead nor steel shall reach him, so
    That it be not the Destined Will.

The thundering line of battle stands,
    And in the air death moans and sings;
But Day shall clasp him with strong hands,
    And Night shall fold him in soft wings.

Julian Grenfell

THE SOLDIER

If I should die, think only this of me :
    That there's some corner of a foreign field
That is for ever England. There shall be
    In that rich earth a richer dust concealed;
A dust whom England bore, shaped, made aware,
Gave, once, her flowers to love, her ways to roam,
A body of England's, breathing English air,
    Washed by the rivers, blest by suns of home.

And think, this heart, all evil shed away,
    A pulse in the eternal mind, no less
    Gives somewhere back the thoughts by England given;
Her sights and sounds; dreams happy as her day;
    And laughter, learnt of friends; and gentleness,
    In hearts at peace, under an English heaven.

Rupert Brooke

FRANCE

She triumphs, in the vivid green
Where sun and quivering foliage meet;
And in each soldier's heart serene;
When death stood near them they have seen
The radiant forests where her feet
Move on a breeze of silver sheen.

And they are fortunate, who fight
For gleaming landscapes swept and shafted
And crowned by cloud pavilions white;
Hearing such harmonies as might
Only from Heaven be downward wafted –
Voices of victory and delight.

Siegfried Sassoon

AT THE WARS

Now that I am ta'en away,
And may not see another day,
What is it to my eye appears?
What sound rings in my stricken ears?
Not even the voice of any friend
Or eyes beloved-world-without-end,
But scenes and sounds of the countryside
In far England across the tide :
An upland field when Spring's begun,
Mellow beneath the evening sun ...
A circle of loose and lichened wall
Over which seven red pines fall ...
An orchard of wizen blossoming trees
Wherein the nesting chaffinches
Begin again the self-same song
All the late April day-time long ...

Paths that lead a shelving course
Between the chalk scarp and the gorse
By English downs; and, O ! too well
I hear the hidden, clanking bell
Of wandering sheep . . . I see the brown
Twilight of the huge empty down . . .
Soon blotted out ! for now a lane
Glitters with warmth of May-time rain,
And on a shooting briar I see
A yellow bird who sings to me.

O yellow-hammer, once I heard
Thy yaffle when no other bird
Could to my sunk heart comfort bring;
But now I would not have thee sing,
So sharp thy note is with the pain
Of England I may not see again !
Yet sing thy song : there answereth
Deep in me a voice which saith :
'The gorse upon the twilit down,
The English loam so sunset brown,
The bowed pines and the sheep-bells' clamour,
The wet, lit lane and the yellow-hammer,
The orchard and the chaffinch song,
Only to the Brave belong.
And he shall lose their joy for aye
If their price he cannot pay,
Who shall find them dearer far
Enriched by blood after long War.'

                                        Robert Nichols

THE DEAD

These hearts were woven of human joys and cares,
　　Washed marvellously with sorrow, swift to mirth.
The years had given them kindness. Dawn was theirs,
　　And sunset, and the colours of the earth.
These had seen movement, and heard music; known
　　Slumber and waking; loved; gone proudly friended;
Felt the quick stir of wonder; sat alone;
　　Touched flowers and furs and cheeks. All this is ended.

There are waters blown by changing winds to laughter
And lit by the rich skies, all day. And after,
　　Frost, with a gesture, stays the waves that dance
And wandering loveliness. He leaves a white
　　Unbroken glory, a gathered radiance,
A width, a shining peace, under the night.

Rupert Brooke

THE DEAD

Blow out, you bugles, over the rich Dead !
　　There's none of these so lonely and poor of old,
　　But, dying, has made us rarer gifts than gold.
These laid the world away; poured out the red
Sweet wine of youth; gave up the years to be
　　Of work and joy, and that unhoped serene,
　　That men called age; and those who would have been,
Their sons, they gave, their immortality.

Blow, bugles, blow ! They brought us, for our dearth,
　　Holiness, lacked so long, and Love, and Pain.
Honour has come back, as a king, to earth,
　　And paid his subjects with a royal wage;
And Nobleness walks in our ways again;
　　And we have come into our heritage.

Rupert Brooke

THE AISNE

We saw fire on the tragic slopes
Where the flood-tide of France's early gain,
Big with wrecked promise and abandoned hopes,
Broke in a surf of blood along the Aisne.

The charge her heroes left us, we assumed,
What, dying, they reconquered, we preserved,
In the chill trenches, harried, shelled, entombed,
Winter came down on us, but no man swerved.

Winter came down on us. The low clouds, torn
In the stark branches of the riven pines,
Blurred the white rockets that from dusk till morn
Traced the wide curve of the close-grappling lines.

In rain, and fog that on the withered hill
Froze before dawn, the lurking foe drew down;
Or light snows fell that made forlorner still
The ravaged country and the ruined town;

Or the long clouds would end. Intensely fair,
The winter constellations blazing forth –
Perseus, the Twins, Orion, the Great Bear –
Gleamed on our bayonets pointing to the north.

And the lone sentinel would start and soar
On wings of strong emotion as he knew
That kinship with the stars that only War
Is great enough to lift man's spirit to.

And ever down the curving front, aglow
With the pale rockets' intermittent light,
He heard, like distant thunder, growl and grow
The rumble of far battles in the night –

Rumours, reverberant, indistinct, remote,
Borne from red fields whose martial names have won
The power to thrill like a far trumpet-note –
Vic, Vailly, Soupir, Hurtelise, Craonne . . .

Craonne, before thy cannon-swept plateau,
Where like sere leaves lay strewn September's dead,
I found for all things I forfeited
A recompense I would not forgo.

For that high fellowship was ours then
With those who, championing another's good,
More than dull Peace or its poor votaries could,
Taught us the dignity of being men.

There we drained deeper the deep cup of life,
And on sublimer summits came to learn,
After soft things, the terrible and stern,
After sweet Love, the majesty of Strife;

There where we faced under those frowning heights
The blast that maims, the hurricane that kills;
There where the watch-lights on the winter hills
Flickered like balefire through inclement nights;

There where, firm links in the unyielding chain,
Where fell the long-planned blow and fell in vain –
Hearts worthy of the honour and the trial,
We helped to hold the lines along the Aisne.

Alan Seeger

RENDEZVOUS

I have a rendezvous with Death
At some disputed barricade,
When Spring comes back with rustling shade
And apple-blossoms fill the air –
I have a rendezvous with Death
When Spring brings back blue days and fair.

It may be he shall take my hand
And lead me into his dark land
And close my eyes and quench my breath –
It may be I shall pass him still.

I have a rendezvous with Death
On some scarred slope of battered hill,
When Spring comes round again this year
And the first meadow-flowers appear.

God knows 'twere better to be deep
Pillowed in silk and scented down,
Where love throbs out in blissful sleep,
Pulse nigh to pulse, and breath to breath,
Where hushed awakenings are dear . . .
But I've a rendezvous with Death
At midnight in some flaming town,
When Spring trips north again this year,
And I to my pledged word am true,
I shall not fail that rendezvous.

Alan Seeger

THE VOLUNTEER

Here lies a clerk who half his life had spent
Toiling at ledgers in a city grey,
Thinking that so his days would drift away
With no lance broken in life's tournament.
Yet ever 'twixt the books and his bright eyes
The gleaming eagles of the legions came,
And horsemen, charging under phantom skies,
Went thundering past beneath the oriflamme.

And now those waiting dreams are satisfied;
From twilight to the halls of dawn he went;
His lance is broken; but he lies content
With that high hour, in which he lived and died.
And falling thus he wants no recompense,
Who found his battle in the last resort;
Nor need he any hearse to bear him hence,
Who goes to join the men of Agincourt.

Herbert Asquith

TO MY BROTHER

Give me your hand, my brother, search my face;
Look in these eyes lest I should think of shame;
For we have made an end of all things base.
We are returning by the road we came.

Your lot is with the ghosts of soldiers dead,
And I am in the field where men must fight.
But in the gloom I see your laurell'd head
And through your victory I shall win the light.

Siegfried Sassoon

IN MEMORIAM S.C.W., V.C.
(8 September 1915)

There is no fitter end than this.
  No need is now to yearn nor sigh.
We know the glory that is his,
  A glory that can never die.

Surely we knew it long before,
  Knew all along that he was made
For a swift radiant morning, for
  A sacrificing swift night-shade.

Charles Sorley

BACK TO REST
*(Composed while marching to Rest Camp after
severe fighting at Loos)*

A leaping wind from England,
   The skies without a stain,
Clean cut against the morning
   Slim poplars after rain,
The foolish noise of sparrows
   And starlings in a wood –
After the grime of battle
   We know that these are good.

Death whining down from Heaven,
   Death roaring from the ground,
Death stinking in the nostril,
   Death shrill in every sound,
Doubting we charged and conquered –
   Hopeless we struck and stood.
Now when the fight is ended
   We know that it was good.

We that have seen the strongest
   Cry like a beaten child,
The sanest eyes unholy,
   The cleanest hands defiled,
We that have known the heart blood
   Less than the lees of wine,
We that have seen men broken,
   We know man is divine.

                 W. N. Hodgson

BEFORE ACTION

By all the glories of the day
  And the cool evening's benison,
By that last sunset touch that lay
  Upon the hills when day was done,
By beauty lavishly outpoured
  And blessings carelessly received,
By all the days that I have lived
  Make me a soldier, Lord.

By all of man's hopes and fears,
  And all the wonders poets sing,
The laughter of unclouded years,
  And every sad and lovely thing;
By the romantic ages stored
  With high endeavour that was his,
By all his mad catastrophes
  Make me a man, O Lord.

I, that on my familiar hill
  Saw with uncomprehending eyes
A hundred of Thy sunsets spill
  Their fresh and sanguine sacrifice,
Ere the sun swings his noonday sword
  Must say goodbye to all of this –
By all delights that I shall miss,
  Help me to die, O Lord.

                    W. N. Hodgson

FOR THE FALLEN

With proud thanksgiving, a mother for her children,
England mourns for her dead across the sea.
Flesh of her flesh they were, spirit of her spirit,
Fallen in the cause of the free.

Solemn the drums thrill : Death august and royal
Sings sorrow up into immortal spheres.
There is music in the midst of desolation
And glory that shines upon our tears.

They went with songs to the battle, they were young,
Straight of limb, true of eye, steady and aglow.
They were staunch to the end against odds uncounted :
They fell with their faces to the foe.

They shall grow not old, as we that are left grow old :
Age shall not weary them, nor the years condemn.
At the going down of the sun and in the morning
We will remember them.

They mingle not with their laughing comrades again;
They sit no more at familiar tables of home;
They have no lot in our labour of the day-time;
They sleep beyond England's foam.

But where our desires are and our hopes profound,
Felt as a well-spring that is hidden from sight,
To the innermost heart of their own land they are known
As the stars are known to the Night;

As the stars that shall be bright when we are dust,
Moving in marches upon the heavenly plain;
As the stars that are starry in the time of our darkness,
To the end, to the end they remain.

Laurence Binyon

By 1915 the war was being fought with a ruthlessness that seemed new and terrible to a world that had not yet heard of Belsen and Hiroshima. As Winston Churchill was later to write in *The World Crisis*:

> Germany having let Hell loose kept well in the van of terror; but she was followed step by step by the desperate and ultimately avenging nations she had assailed. Every outrage against humanity or international law was repaid by reprisals often on a greater scale and of longer duration. When all was over, Torture and Cannibalism were the only two expedients that the civilized, scientific, Christian States had been able to deny themselves, and these were of doubtful utility.

In 1915 both sides began to realize how terrific and inexhaustible were the sheer powers of destruction that they were deploying. Also, both sides began to doubt whether there was any hope of either gaining a swift victory. The precise state that Germany, Britain and France had reached in the development of scientific weapons meant that a deadlock existed in the west by land and sea. As for the naval war, the German fleet stayed in its harbours and the British Admiralty had no way of enticing it out to give battle; but, while it stayed in being, the main British fleet had to be at instant readiness in Scapa Flow in case it came out. On land the Germans had built a long line of trenches from the North Sea to the Alps, and had armed them with enough barbed wire and machine guns to make them impregnable. The best plan for the Allies would have been to postpone any major attack until they had built new weapons, such as tanks, or until their blockade had sapped German morale. Instead, in 1915, 1916, and 1917 the British and French generals threw away lives on an extravagant scale by mounting one massive, futile frontal attack after another. Meanwhile in 1915 the Allies tried to out-manoeuvre the Germans by landing troops on the shores of the Dardanelles, part of Turkey in Europe. But this plan failed completely because it was mismanaged in detail.

As more and more intelligent English soldiers began to experience on the Western Front the grim horrors and immeasurable discomforts of trench warfare, and as they began to doubt the wisdom of the tactics that led to the unsuccessful attacks of 1915 (e.g. by the British at Loos in the late autumn), their poetry began to ask disconcerting questions or to express inescapable doubts. Soldiers, especially young soldiers, began to lose faith in the British caste system that promoted generals according to the school they went to, rather than to their ability; soldiers began to feel themselves a race apart from the civilians at home, who were making a profit out of the war and were enjoying the second-hand excitement of following battles in the newspapers; and they began to lose faith in God who permitted these things to happen.

As early as August 1914 the atheist A. E. Housman had praised the men who died at Mons for having defended 'What God abandoned'. As the carnage grew and as more and more people realized how brutalizing were many aspects of army life, others began to wonder whether God could exist at all; if there was a God, surely he would not allow such horrors. In July 1915 Sorley, who was one of the first poets to feel the widening gulf between the civilians at home and the men in the trenches, wrote two sonnets about death which quite ignore Christianity. His bleak imagery of 'the broken pail' and 'the clean slate' pictured Death as the complete end of everything. He is not only giving deliberately a very different picture of Death from the picture that Brooke gave; he is also foreseeing the huge scale of the tragedy which directly or indirectly was to overwhelm twenty-five million people.

Sassoon in 'The Redeemer' still thinks of an ordinary English soldier as a second Christ, and still assumes that God is completely on the English side, but he introduces a new type of sordid realism into the descriptions of trench warfare that accompany his theological images. R. E. Vernède in 'A Listening Post' voices the hesitant uncertainty about Christianity that later characterizes much of Owen's poetry. He finds it strange that a bird should sit and sing while men—presumably higher animals made in the image of God—are planning the murder of their fellow men. He hopes that *maybe* God will bring forth some new harmony out of war's discord, but he does not sound at all sure.

E. A. Mackintosh in 'Recruiting' still assumes that every manly 'lad' will go to share the 'martyrdom' and 'sacrifice', but he is contemptuously satirical—in the way that Sassoon's later poetry will be—of the insincere propagandists, the vulgar women, the dishonest journalists and the smug civilians at home. He believes that their cheap glibness disgraces the noble causes that they claim to advance. Wilfred Owen's 'Exposure' was written as late as February 1917, but it speaks out the feelings of someone who has recently reached the front line for the first time and whose Christian assumptions have been savagely challenged.

The following section of this anthology expresses the feelings of men who have begun to doubt most orthodox assumptions about war, society and religion, but have not been driven very far yet.

These poets felt that Christianity had so far failed to explain or justify the enormous scale of the slaughter, and the terrible indignities to which war subjected individuals as they died.

EPITAPH ON AN ARMY OF MERCENARIES

These, in the day when heaven was falling,
    The hour when earth's foundations fled,
Followed their mercenary calling
    And took their wages and are dead.

Their shoulders held the sky suspended;
    They stood, and earth's foundations stay;
What God abandoned, these defended,
    And saved the sum of things for pay.

                                    A. E. Housman

TWO SONNETS
(12 June 1915)

I

Saints have adored the lofty soul of you.
   Poets have whitened at your high renown.
We stand among the many millions who
   Do hourly wait to pass your pathway down.
You, so familiar, once were strange : we tried
   To live as of your presence unaware.
But now in every road on every side
   We see your straight and steadfast signpost there.

I think it like that signpost in my land,
   Hoary and tall, which pointed me to go
Upward, into the hills, on the right hand,
   Where the mists swim and the winds shriek and blow,
A homeless land and friendless, but a land
   I did not know and that I wished to know.

II

Such, such is Death : no triumph : no defeat :
   Only an empty pail, a slate rubbed clean,
   A merciful putting away of what has been.

And this we know : Death is not Life effete,
   Life crushed, the broken pail. We who have seen
   So marvellous things know well the end not yet.

Victor and vanquished are a-one in death :
   Coward and brave : friend, foe. Ghosts do not say
'Come, what was your record when you drew breath?'
   But a big blot has hid each yesterday
So poor, so manifestly incomplete.
   And your bright Promise, withered long and sped,
Is touched, stirs, rises, opens and grows sweet
   And blossoms and is you, when you are dead.

Charles Sorley

THE SOWER
(Eastern France)

Familiar, year by year, to the creaking wain
Is the long road's level ridge above the plain.
Today a battery comes with horses and guns
On the straight road, that under the poplars runs,
At leisurely pace, the guns with mouths declined,
Harness merrily ringing, and dust behind.
Makers of widows, makers of orphans, they
Pass to their burial business, alert and gay.

But down in the field, where sun has the furrow dried,
Is a man who walks in the furrow with even stride.
At every step, with elbow jerked across,
He scatters seed in a quick, deliberate toss,
The immemorial gesture of Man confiding
To Earth, that restores tenfold in a season's gliding.
He is grave and patient, sowing his children's bread :
He treads the kindly furrow, nor turns his head.

Laurence Binyon

THE EBB OF WAR

In the seven-times taken and re-taken town
Peace ! The mind stops; sense argues against sense.
The August sun is ghostly in the street
As if the Silence of a thousand years
Were its familiar. All is as it was
At the instant of the shattering : flat-thrown walls;
Dislocated rafters; lintels blown awry
And toppling over; what were windows, mere
Gapings on mounds of dust and shapelessness;
Charred posts caught in a bramble of twisted iron;
Wires sagging tangled across the street; the black
Skeleton of a vine, wrenched from the old house
It clung to; a limp bell-pull; here and there
Little printed papers pasted on the wall.

It is like a madness crumpled up in stone,
Laughterless, tearless, meaningless; a frenzy
Stilled, like at ebb the shingle in sea-caves
Where the imagined weight of water swung
Its senseless crash with pebbles in myriads churned
By the random seethe. But here was flesh and blood,
Seeing eyes, feeling nerves; memoried minds
With the habit of the picture of these fields
And the white roads crossing the wide green plain,
All vanished ! One could fancy the very fields
Were memory's projection, phantoms ! All
Silent ! The stone is hot to the touching hand.
Footsteps come strange to the sense. In the sloped churchyard,
Where the tower shows the blue through its great rents,
Shadow falls over pitiful wrecked graves,
And on the gravel a bare-headed boy,
Hands in his pockets, with large absent eyes,
Whistles the Marseillaise : To Arms, To Arms !
There is no other sound in the bright air.
It is as if they heard under the grass,
The dead men of the Marne, and their thin voice
Used those young lips to sing it from their graves,
The song that sang a nation into arms.
And far away to the listening ear in the silence
Like remote thunder throb the guns of France.

Laurence Binyon

THE REDEEMER

Darkness : the rain sluiced down; the mire was deep;
It was past twelve on a mid-winter night,
When peaceful folk in beds lay snug asleep;
There, with much work to do before the light,
We lugged our clay-sucked boots as best we might
Along the trench; sometimes a bullet sang,
And droning shells burst with a hollow bang;
We were soaked, chilled and wretched, every one;
Darkness; the distant wink of a huge gun.

I turned in the black ditch, loathing the storm;
A rocket fizzed and burned with blanching flare,
And lit the face of what had been a form
Floundering in mirk. He stood before me there;
I say that He was Christ; stiff in the glare,
And leaning forward from His burdening task,
Both arms supporting it; His eyes on mine
Stared from the woeful head that seemed a mask
Of mortal pain in Hell's unholy shine.

No thorny crown, only a woollen cap
He wore—an English soldier, white and strong,
Who loved his time like any simple chap,
Good days of work and sport and homely song;
Now he has learned that nights are very long,
And dawn a watching of the windowed sky.
But to the end, unjudging, he'll endure
Horror and pain, not uncontent to die
That Lancaster on Lune may stand secure.

He faced me, reeling in his weariness,
Shouldering his load of planks, so hard to bear.
I say that He was Christ, who wrought to bless
All groping things with freedom bright as air,
And with His mercy washed and made them fair.
Then the flame sank, and all grew black as pitch,
While we began to struggle along the ditch;
And someone flung his burden in the muck,
Mumbling : 'O Christ Almighty, now I'm stuck !'

Siegfried Sassoon

A LISTENING POST

The sun's a red ball in the oak
    And all the grass is grey with dew,
A while ago a blackbird spoke –
    He didn't know the world's askew.

And yonder rifleman and I
    Wait here behind the misty trees
To shoot the first man that goes by,
    Our rifles ready on our knees.

How could he know that if we fail
    The world may lie in chains for years
And England be a bygone tale
    And right be wrong, and laughter tears?

Strange that this bird sits there and sings
    While we must only sit and plan –
Who are so much the higher thing –
    The murder of our fellow man . . .

But maybe God will cause to be –
    Who brought forth sweetness from the strong –
Out of our discords harmony
    Sweeter than that bird's song.

                    R. E. Vernède

RECRUITING

'Lads, you're wanted, go and help',
On the railway carriage wall
Stuck the poster, and I thought
Of the hands that penned the call.

Fat civilians wishing they
'Could go and fight the Hun'.
Can't you see them thanking God
That they're over forty-one?

Girls with feathers, vulgar songs –
Washy verse on England's need –
God – and don't we damned well know
How the message ought to read.

'Lads, you're wanted! over there',
Shiver in the morning dew,
More poor devils like yourselves
Waiting to be killed by you.

Go and help to swell the names
In the casualty lists.
Help to make a column's stuff
For the blasted journalists.

Help to keep them nice and safe
From the wicked German foe.
Don't let him come over here!
'Lads, you're wanted – out you go.'

    *   *   *

There's a better word than that,
Lads, and can't you hear it come
From a million men that call
You to share their martyrdom?

Leave the harlots still to sing
Comic songs about the Hun,
Leave the fat old men to say
Now *we've* got them on the run.

Better twenty honest years
Then their dull three score and ten.
Lads, you're wanted. Come and learn
To live and die with honest men.

You shall learn what men can do
If you will but pay the price,
Learn the gaiety and strength
In the gallant sacrifice.

Take your risk of life and death
Underneath the open sky.
Live clean or go out quick –
Lads, you're wanted. Come and die.

                    E. A. *Mackintosh*

EXPOSURE

Our brains ache, in the merciless iced east winds that knive us . . .
Wearied we keep awake because the night is silent . . .
Low, drooping flares confuse our memories of the salient . . .
Worried by silence, sentries whisper, curious, nervous,
        But nothing happens.

Watching, we hear the mad gusts tugging on the wire,
Like twitching agonies of men among its brambles.
Northward, incessantly, the flickering gunnery rumbles,
Far off, like a dull rumour of some other war.
        What are we doing here?

The poignant misery of dawn begins to grow . . .
We only know war lasts, rain soaks, and clouds sag stormy.
Dawn massing in the east her melancholy army
Attacks once more in ranks on shivering ranks of grey,
        But nothing happens.

Sudden successive flights of bullets streak the silence.
Less deathly than the air that shudders black with snow,
With sidelong flowing flakes that flock, pause, and renew;
We watch them wandering up and down the wind's nonchalance,
        But nothing happens.

Pale flakes with fingering stealth come feeling for our faces –
We cringe in holes, back on forgotten dreams, and stare, snowdazed,
Deep into grassier ditches. So we drowse, sun-dozed,
Littered with blossoms trickling where the blackbird fusses.
   Is it that we are dying?

Slowly our ghosts drag home : glimpsing the sunk fires, glozed
With crusted dark-red jewels; crickets jingle there;
For hours the innocent mice rejoice : the house is theirs;
Shutters and doors, all closed : on us the doors are closed –
   We turn back to our dying.

Since we believe not otherwise can kind fires burn;
Nor ever suns smile true on child, or field, or fruit.
For God's invincible spring our love is made afraid;
Therefore, not loath, we lie out here; therefore were born,
   For love of God seems dying.

Tonight, His frost will fasten on this mud and us,
Shrivelling many hands, puckering foreheads crisp.
The burying-party, picks and shovels in their shaking grasp,
Pause over half-known faces. All their eyes are ice,
   But nothing happens.
                                   Wilfred Owen

By the late autumn of 1914 the war of movement in France had virtually ended, and it did not begin again until March 1918. Throughout 1915, 1916, and 1917 the English and French mounted a series of offensives against the Germans which achieved minute gains in ground at the cost of appalling casualties. Trenches, barbed wire, pill-boxes and machine guns combined to form impregnable defences, whenever they were manned by resolute troops, with the result that the attackers always lost more heavily than the defenders. In these years—1915, 1916, 1917—nearly three Allied soldiers died for every German they killed. While the Germans remained on the defensive in the West they were able to advance, in the East, deep into the territory of Russia, Roumania, and Serbia—ultimately knocking the first two countries out of the war. But in 1918 the war took a very different turn; Ludendorff, the German commander, delivered in March 1918 a major assault in the West which was intended to win the war before the Americans could invervene in force. It gained a large area of territory by the standards of warfare in 1915–17, but it inflicted on the advancing Germans casualties from which they never recovered. Moreover the Allies, after stopping the German advance, improved their organization, weapons and tactics; in consequence Foch and Haig directed the Allied advance in 1918 more skilfully than Allied commanders, especially Haig, had done before.

Britain's first major bloodbath on the Western Front, in the 1915–17 series of unsuccessful attacks that wasted Allied lives, occurred in September 1915 when Sir John French attacked at Loos. On 1 July 1916, Haig repeated this tragic error on a far larger scale. His assault in the valley of the Somme was preceded by a week's artillery bombardment on an unprecedented scale. But though this was intended to overwhelm the German defenders, it robbed the attack of all element of surprise. On the first day British casualties were appalling; 60,000 men, the best of Britain's youth, were mown down by German machine-guns. For the first time the hundreds of thousands of young men who had volunteered in 1914 and 1915 were considered sufficiently trained to be used on a massive scale against the Germans; their youth and bravery were just thrown away. Like the General in Sassoon's poem, Haig

did for them . . . by his plan of attack.

The next four months of fighting on the Somme led to 420,000 casualties yet gained very little ground.

The costliest attack of 1917, the Third Battle of Ypres, took place in the low-lying waterlogged fields of Ypres and Passchendaele. From July to December 1917 Haig amassed so huge a force of artillery that the sound of the guns could be heard in Surrey, but casualties mounted to 300,000 as Haig refused to admit that the torrential rain gave the Germans, on the higher ground, a deadly advantage. Wounded British soldiers were drowned in waterlogged shellholes or suffocated in mud.

War of this sort was utterly different from the war that Brooke had looked forward to. The soldier-poets who endured its ugly horrors wrote down their own honest reactions to it, partly in order to find some relief for their feelings, and partly to tell the civilians at home what war was really like. They felt that they owed it to their dead comrades to let the public, the world and posterity know what unspeakable horrors war inflicted on the front-line troops. The poets were more articulate than their fellow soldiers; they set out to tell the world about the lice, cold, hunger, sleeplessness, fear, misery and stench that were inherent in modern war. One thing that especially appalled them was the huge scale of modern war, which decreed that whether an individual survived an artillery bombardment depended on chance and not on his bravery or skill. Some of them seem to have hoped—rather optimistically—that if only mankind learnt the truth about death and mutilation in battle, they would avoid war as too horrible to continue.

Robert Graves was one of the first poets to dwell, in 'A Dead Boche', on the loathsome physical facts of death in battle. He begins :

I'll say (you've heard it said before)
War's Hell ! and if you doubt the same,
Today I found in Mametz Wood
A certain cure for lust of blood.

He then goes on to describe in detail the repellent appearance of the corpse. Graves is setting out to destroy in his readers all unreal ideas that war is a romantic, chivalric tournament in which the disembodied slain go 'to join the dead of Agincourt'. Wilfred Owen's letters reflect a similar reaction; they paint graphic pictures of the no man's

land in the winter of 1916–17 as it appeared to a sensitive young
officer seeing it for the first time :

> It is like the eternal place of gnashing of teeth : the Slough of
> Despond could be contained in one of its crater-holes; the fires of
> Sodom and Gomorrah could not light a candle to it—to find the
> way to Babylon the Fallen. It is pock-marked like a body of foulest
> disease, and its odour is the breath of cancer. I have not seen any
> dead. I have done worse. In the dank air I have *perceived* it, and in
> the darkness, *felt*. No Man's Land under snow is like the face of
> the moon, chaotic, crater-ridden, uninhabitable, awful, the abode
> of madness. To call it 'England' ! I would as soon call my house
> Krupp Villa, or my child Chlorina-Phosgena . . . The people of
> England needn't hope. They must agitate. But they are not yet
> agitated even. Let them imagine 50 strong men trembling as with
> ague for 50 hours !

The effect of such ordeals on the spirit of the men was terrible. Even
behind the lines Owen found that :

> Everything is makeshift. The English seem to have fallen into the
> French unhappy-go-lucky non-system. There are scarcely any houses
> here. The men lie in barns. Our Mess Room is also an Ante and
> Orderly Room. We eat and drink out of old tins, some of which
> show traces of ancient enamel. We are never dry, and never 'off
> duty'. On all the officer's faces there is a harassed look that I have
> never seen before, and which in England never will be seen—out of
> the jails. The men are just as Bairnsfather has them—expressionless
> lumps.

Sassoon makes more systematic use of this aggressive realism in his
poetry than ever Graves or Owen did. He protests against the bizarre
indignities which war inflicts on the corpses of the dead. 'The Rear-
guard' tells the story of how a normally decent officer kicks a recum-
bent figure, which he first imagines to be a sleeping British soldier but
ultimately recognizes as a corpse. Sassoon does not *underline* the
moral; he leaves it for the reader to draw for himself, which is unusual
with Sassoon, whose protests against the horror of war are sometimes
too obvious and emphatic. The grim moral is that war corrupts all
who take part in it; for the nervous tension of a long spell in the front
line has made the officer in the poem callous, bad-tempered and
viciously impatient. The fact that he has not slept for days is intended
by Sassoon to seem an inadequate excuse for such callousness.

However, it is interesting to see how Sassoon retold the same story in his semi-autobiographical prose book *Memoirs of an Infantry Officer*; there he plays down the horrific element in the story: he omits details such as the corpse's blackening wound; he also stresses that it was a German corpse that was killed, whereas the poem suggests that it was British. The poem, much more than the prose account, stresses how war robs a dead man of all dignity and a living man of all humanity.

Other of Sassoon's poems stress the aspects of war that demoralize soldiers, such as the terrible suspense of waiting for zero hour:

> Lines of grey, muttering faces, masked with fear,
> They leave their trenches, going over the top,
> While time ticks bleak and busy on their wrists,
> And hope, with furtive eyes and grappling fists,
> Flounders in mud.

These haggard, hopeless soldiers seem to live in a stricken world that has been overwhelmed by some unspeakable disaster.

Of course, too much obsession with distasteful details of death and corruption defeats the purpose of poetry. A poet may wish to shock or to horrify, but he must not repel us. Clearly some readers have found that Sassoon's insistence on gruesome details defeats his own purpose; the present editor does not find Sassoon's poetry too gruesome, but he does find that some poems, notably 'God, How I Hate You', and 'Night Patrol' by Arthur Graeme West are too nauseating to be classed as poetry.

Blunden's descriptive poems impress on their readers the grotesque horror of war without ever needing to become over-emphatic. He shows how the natural beauty of Belgium and France has been destroyed by the unnatural devastation of war. Under the full moon the ravaged landscape of Ypres seems to belong to a sinister, alien world where Nature's perverse vitality oddly preserves a little of the original beauty. Blunden also analyses the effects of these scenes of horror on the soldiers who observe them; and in poems such as 'Pillbox' and 'The Welcome' he stresses the irrationality of war which brings death where one would least expect it.

Wilfred Owen was also resolved to be realistic, though it is noticeable that his most aggressively realistic poems are not his best. Like Sassoon he explains that each individual can stand so much of the front line and no more. He does not blame the young lad who commits suicide because:

Courage leaked, as sand
From the best sand-bags after years of rain.

He dwells on the horrible details of deaths and terrible physical effects
of wounds. 'Dulce et Decorum est' sets out to shock civilians with un-
relenting details of a man's death from gas, which was 'obscene as
cancer'. In a number of minor poems Owen writes like a talented
imitator of Sassoon, rather than in the distinctive style that he made
his own. In these he sets out to shock his reader by stressing the ugly
truths about war. 'The Sentry' tells us about one soldier who is tem-
porarily blinded by shell-shock and another who wants to drown
himself. 'A Terre' dwells on the wounded soldier who is blind and
semi-paralysed. 'Disabled' gives a grim picture of the legless, armless
victim :

Now he will never feel again how slim
Girls' waists are, or how warm their subtle hands;
All of them touch him like some queer disease.

'Mental Cases' harps on the horrifying appearance of the deranged
soldiers whose 'minds' the dead have ravished. When, like Blunden,
Owen gives us a graphic description of how war has disfigured the
landscape, he sees a very grim scene indeed :

A sad land, weak with sweats of dearth,
Gray, cratered like the moon with hollow woe,
And pitted with great pocks and scabs of plagues.

Rosenberg in some ways paints the grimmest scene of all these
realists. 'Returning, We Hear the Larks' uses the incongruous beauty
of the larks' song to emphasize by contrast the ugliness of the 'poison-
blasted track' along which Rosenberg and his fellow soldiers drag their
'anguished limbs'. 'Louse Hunting' is as uncompromising a poem as its
title suggests; it presents a grotesque picture of soldiers tearing at their
shirts, and even setting fire to them by accident, in a mad rage to
'hurt the verminous brood'. 'Break of Day in the Trenches' concen-
trates on the rats and the poppy who outlive, in 'the torn fields of
France', the strongest human athletes. 'Dead Man's Dump' just man-
ages to stop short of becoming nauseating, but it dwells on the corpses
that are crushed further into the earth by the ration-cart lumbering
over them. The title stresses the contemptuous indifference with
which modern warfare treats these corpses. The last lines describe how
the mules drag the ration-limber over the dying man at the exact

moment of death; in this way Rosenberg stresses how helpless and ignominious the individual seems when overwhelmed by modern war. The photographic details of his description of the battlefield imply the conclusion that Sassoon stated more bluntly to Robert Nichols:

War is hell and those who institute it are criminals.

NOON

It is midday : the deep trench glares . . .
A buzz and blaze of flies . . .
The hot wind puffs the giddy airs . . .
The great sun rakes the skies.

No sound in all the stagnant trench
Where forty standing men
Endure the sweat and grit and stench,
Like cattle in a pen.

Sometimes a sniper's bullet whirs
Or twangs the whining wire;
Sometimes a soldier sighs and stirs
As in hell's frying fire.

From out a high cool cloud descends
An aeroplane's far moan . . .
The sun strikes down, the thin cloud rends . . .
The black spot travels on.

And sweating, dizzied, isolate
In the hot trench beneath,
We bide the next shrewd move of fate
Be it of life or death.

Robert Nichols

COMRADES: AN EPISODE

Before, before he was aware
The 'Verey' light had risen . . . on the air
It hung glistering . . .

               And he could not stay his hand
From moving to the barbed wire's broken strand.
A rifle cracked.

          He fell.
Night waned. He was alone. A heavy shell
Whispered itself passing high, high overhead.
His wound was wet to his hand : for still it bled
On to the glimmering ground.
Then with a slow, vain smile his wound he bound,
Knowing, of course, he'd not see home again –
Home whose thought he put away.

                  His men
Whispered : 'Where's Mister Gates?' 'Out on the wire.'
'I'll get him', said one . . .

             Dawn blinked, and the fire
Of the Germans heaved up and down the line.
'Stand to !'

         Too late ! 'I'll get him.' 'O the swine !
When we might get him in yet safe and whole !'
'Corporal didn't see 'un fall out on patrol,
Or he'd 'a got 'un.' 'Sssh !'

            'No talking there.'
A whisper : ''A went down at the last flare.'
Meanwhile the Maxims toc-toc-tocked; their swish
Of bullets told death lurked against the wish.
No hope for him !

         His corporal, as one shamed,
Vainly and helplessly his ill-lucked blamed.

Then Gates slowly saw the morn
Break in a rosy peace through the lone thorn
By which he lay, and felt the dawn-wind pass
Whispering through the pallid, stalky grass
Of No-Man's Land . . .

And the tears came
Scaldingly sweet, more lovely than a flame.
He closed his eyes : he thought of home
And grit his teeth. He knew no help could come . . .

The silent sun over the earth held sway,
Occasional rifles cracked and far away
A heedless speck, a 'plane, slid on alone,
Like a fly traversing a cliff of stone.
'I must get back', said Gates aloud, and heaved
At his body. But it lay bereaved
Of any power. He could not wait till night . . .
And he lay still. Blood swam across his sight.
Then with a groan :
'No luck ever ! Well, I must die alone.'

Occasional rifles cracked. A cloud that shone,
Gold-rimmed, blackened the sun and then was gone . . .
The sun still smiled. The grass sang in its play.
Someone whistled : 'Over the hills and far away'.
Gates watched silently the swift, swift sun
Burning his life before it was begun . . .

Suddenly he heard Corporal Timmins' voice : 'Now then,
'Urry up with that tea.'
                                        'Hi Ginger !' 'Bill !' His men !
Timmins and Jones and Wilkinson (the 'bard'),
And Hughes and Simpson. It was hard
Not to see them : Wilkinson, stubby, grim,
With his 'No, sir,' 'Yes, sir,' and the slim
Simpson : 'Indeed, sir?' (while it seemed he winked
Because his smiling left eye always blinked)
And Corporal Timmins, straight and blond and wise,
With his quiet-scanning, level, hazel eyes;
And all the others . . . tunics that didn't fit . . .
A dozen different sorts of eyes. O it
Was hard to lie there ! Yet he must. But no :
'I've got to die. I'll get to them. I'll go'.

Inch by inch he fought, breathless and mute,
Dragging his carcase like a famished brute . . .
His head was hammering, and his eyes were dim;
A bloody sweat seemed to ooze out of him
And freeze along his spine . . . Then he'd lie still
Before another effort of his will
Took him one nearer yard.

      The parapet was reached.
He could not rise to it. A lookout screeched :
'Mr Gates !'

    Three figures in one breath
Leaped up. Two figures fell in toppling death;
And Gates was lifted in. 'Who's hit?' said he.
'Timmins and Jones.' 'Why did they that for me? –
I'm gone already !' Gently they laid him prone
And silently watched.

     He twitched. They heard him moan

'Why for me?' His eyes roamed round, and none replied.
'I see it was alone I should have died.'
They shook their heads. Then, 'Is the doctor here?'
'He's coming, sir; he's hurryin', no fear.'
'No good . . .

    Lift me.' They lifted him.
He smiled and held his arms out to the dim,
And in a moment passed beyond their ken,
Hearing him whisper, 'O my men, my men !'

         Robert Nichols

BREAKFAST

We ate our breakfast lying on our backs
Because the shells were screeching overhead.
I bet a rasher to a loaf of bread
That Hull United would beat Halifax
When Jimmy Stainthorpe played full-back instead
Of Billy Bradford. Ginger raised his head
And cursed, and took the bet, and dropt back dead.
We ate our breakfast lying on our backs
Because the shells were screeching overhead.

Wilfrid Gibson

WINTER WARFARE

Colonel Cold strode up the Line
   (Tabs of rime and spurs of ice).
Stiffened all where he did glare,
   Horses, men, and lice.

Visited a forward post,
   Left them burning, ear to foot;
Fingers stuck to biting steel,
   Toes to frozen boot.

Stalked on into No Man's Land,
   Turned the wire to fleecy wool,
Iron stakes to sugar sticks
   Snapping at a pull.

Those who watched with hoary eyes
   Saw two figures gleaming there;
Hauptman Kälte, Colonel Cold,
   Gaunt, in the grey air.

Stiffly, tinkling spurs they moved
   Glassy eyed, with glinting heel
Stabbing those who lingered there
   Torn by screaming steel.

Edgell Rickword

GOING INTO THE LINE
At 3.15, No 11 Platoon, 100 yards in rear of No 10,
will move from Pommiers Redoubt.

So soon !
At 3.15. And would return here . . . when?
It didn't say. Who would return? P'raps all,
P'raps none. Then it had come at last !
It had come at last ! his own stupendous hour,
Long waited, dreaded, almost hoped-for too,
When all else seemed the foolery of power;
It had come at last ! and suddenly the world
Was sharply cut in two. On one side lay
A golden, dreamy, peaceful afternoon,
And on the other, men gone made with fear,
A hell of noise and darkness, a Last Day
Daily enacted. Now good-bye to one
And to the other . . . well, acceptance : that
At least he'd give; many had gone with joy :
He loathed it from his very inmost soul.

The golden world ! It lay just over there,
Peacefully dreaming. In its clear bright depths
Friends moved – he saw them going here and there,
Like thistledown above an August meadow :
Gently as in a gentle dream they moved,
Unagonized, unwrought, nor sad, nor proud,
Faces he loved to agony – and none
Could see, or know, or bid him well-adieu.
Blasphemous irony ! To think how oft
On such a day a friend would hold his hand
Saying good-bye, though they would meet next day,
And now . . . He breathed his whole soul out,
Bidding it span the unbridged senseless miles
And glow about their thoughts in waves of love.

'Twas time already ! Now? As soon as this?
Did his voice hold? How did he look to them?
Poor craven little crowd of human mites !
Now they were crawling over the scarred cheese,
Silently going towards that roaring sea,
Each thinking his own thought, craving perhaps

A body that would fail, or with set teeth
Pitting a human will against the world.
Now every step seemed an eternity :
Each stretch of earth unreachable until it lay
Behind and a stretch longer lay beyond.
Would it never be ended? Crumbling earth,
Dry with the cracks of earthquake, dumbly showed
Death had just trodden there – and there he lay,
Foully deformed in what was once a man.
'Lo ! as these are, so shalt thou be', he thought,
Shuddered : then thrilled almost to ecstasy,
As one from hell delivered up to heaven.

How slow they moved in front ! Yes, slower still.
Then we must stop : we were not eighty yards.
But to stop here – to wait for it ! Oh no !
Backward or forward, anything but not stop –
Not stand and wait ! There's no alternative.
And now he rasps out, 'Halt !' They stand and curse,
Eyes furtive, fingers moving senselessly.
There comes a roar nearer and louder till
His head is bursting with noise and the earth shakes.
'A bloody near one, that !' and 'What the hell
Are we stuck here for?' come with sudden growls.
He moves without a word, and on they trudge.
So near ! Yet nothing ! Then how long? How long? . . .

And slowly in his overheated mind
Peace like a river through the desert flows,
And sweetness wells and overflows in streams
That reach the farthest friend in memory.
Peace now, and dear delight in serving these,
These poor sheep, driven innocent to death :
Peace undisturbed, though the poor senses jump,
And horror catches at the heart as when
Death unsuspected flaunts his grisly hand
Under the very eye of quietness :
Peace, peace with all, even the enemy,
Compassion for them deep as for his own :
Quietness now amid the thunderous noise,
And sweet elation in the grave of gloom.

Max Plowman

DREAMERS

Soldiers are citizens of death's grey land,
    Drawing no dividend from time's tomorrows.
In the great hour of destiny they stand,
    Each with his feuds, and jealousies, and sorrows.
Soldiers are sworn to action; they must win
    Some flaming, fatal climax with their lives.
Soldiers are dreamers; when the guns begin
    They think of firelit homes, clean beds and wives.

I see them in foul dug-outs, gnawed by rats,
    And in the ruined trenches, lashed with rain,
Dreaming of things they did with balls and bats,
    And mocked by hopeless longing to regain
Bank-holidays, and picture shows, and spats,
    And going to the office in the train.

Siegfried Sassoon

THE REAR-GUARD
(Hindenburg Line, April 1917)

Groping along the tunnel, step by step,
He winked his prying torch with patching glare
From side to side, and sniffed the unwholesome air.

Tins, boxes, bottles, shapes too vague to know;
A mirror smashed, the mattress from a bed;
And he, exploring fifty feet below
The rosy gloom of battle overhead.

Tripping, he grabbed the wall; saw someone lie
Humped at his feet, half-hidden by a rug,
And stooped to give the sleeper's arm a tug.
'I'm looking for headquarters.' No reply.
'God blast your neck !' (For days he'd had no sleep,)
'Get up and guide me through this stinking place.'

Savage, he kicked a soft, unanswering heap,
And flashed his beam across the livid face
Terribly glaring up, whose eyes yet wore
Agony dying hard ten days before;
And fists of fingers clutched a blackening wound.

Alone he staggered on until he found
Dawn's ghost that filtered down a shafted stair
To the dazed, muttering creatures underground
Who hear the boom of shells in muffled sound.
At last, with sweat of horror in his hair,
He climbed through darkness to the twilight air,
Unloading hell behind him step by step.

                              Siegfried Sassoon

SPRING OFFENSIVE

Halted against the shade of a last hill,
They fed, and lying easy, were at ease
And, finding comfortable chests and knees,
Carelessly slept. But many there stood still
To face the stark, blank sky beyond the ridge,
Knowing their feet had come to the end of the world.

Marvelling they stood, and watched the long grass swirled
By the May breeze, murmurous with wasp and midge,
For though the summer oozed into their veins
Like an injected drug for their bodies' pains,
Sharp on their souls hung the imminent line of grass,
Fearfully flashed the sky's mysterious glass.

Hour after hour they ponder the warm field –
And the far valley behind, where the buttercup
Had blessed with gold their slow boots coming up,
Where even the little brambles would not yield,
But clutched and clung to them like sorrowing hands;
They breathe like trees unstirred.

Till like a cold gust thrills the little word
At which each body and its soul begird
And tighten them for battle. No alarms
Of bugles, no high flags, no clamorous haste –
Only a lift and flare of eyes that faced
The sun, like a friend with whom their love is done.
O larger shone that smile against the sun –
Mightier than His whose bounty these have spurned.

So, soon they topped the hill, and raced together
Over an open stretch of herb and heather
Exposed. And instantly the whole sky burned
With fury against them; earth set sudden cups
In thousands for their blood; and the green slope
Chasmed and steepened sheer to infinite space.

*   *   *

Of them who running on that last high place
Leapt to swift unseen bullets, or went up
On the hot blast and fury of hell's upsurge,
Or plunged and fell away past this world's verge,
Some say God caught them even before they fell.

But what say such as from existence' brink
Ventured but drave too swift to sink,
The few who rushed in the body to enter hell,
And there out-fiending all its fiends and flames
With superhuman inhumanities,
Long-famous glories, immemorial shames –
And crawling slowly back, have by degrees
Regained cool peaceful air in wonder –
Why speak not they of comrades that went under?

                                    Wilfred Owen

DULCE ET DECORUM EST

Bent double, like old beggars under sacks,
Knock-kneed, coughing like hags, we cursed through sludge,
Till on the haunting flares we turned our backs,
And towards our distant rest began to trudge.
Men marched asleep. Many had lost their boots,
But limped on, blood-shod. All went lame; all blind;
Drunk with fatigue; deaf even to the hoots
Of gas-shells dropping softly behind.

Gas ! Gas ! Quick, boys ! – An ecstasy of fumbling,
Fitting the clumsy helmets just in time;
But someone still was yelling out and stumbling
And floundering like a man in fire or lime –
Dim, through the misty panes and thick green light,
As under a green sea, I saw him drowning.

In all my dreams, before my helpless sight,
He plunges at me, guttering, choking, drowning.

If in some smothering dreams, you too could pace
Behind the wagon that we flung him in,
And watch the white eyes writhing in his face,
His hanging face, like a devil's sick of sin;
If you could hear, at every jolt, the blood
Come gargling from the froth-corrupted lungs,
Obscene as cancer, bitter as the cud
Of vile, incurable sores on innocent tongues –
My friend, you would not tell with such high zest
To children ardent for some desperate glory,
The old Lie : Dulce et decorum est
Pro patria mori.

                              Wilfred Owen

CLEAR WEATHER

A cloudless day ! with a keener line
   The ruins jut on the glittering blue,
The gas gongs by the billets shine
   Like gold or wine, so trim and new.

Sharp through the wreckage pries the gust,
   And down the roads where wheels have rolled
Whirls the dry snow in powdery dust,
   And starlings muster ruffled with cold.

The gunners profit by the light,
   The guns like surly bandogs bark;
And toward Saint Jean in puffs of white
   The anti-aircraft find a mark.

And now the sentries' whistles ply,
   For overhead with whirring drone
An Albatross comes racing by,
   Immensely high, and one of our own.

From underneath to meet it mounts,
   And banks and spirals up, and straight
The popping maxims' leaden founts
   Spurt fire, the Boche drops like a weight :

A hundred feet he nose-dives, then
   He rights himself and scuds down sky
Towards the German lines again,
   A great transparent dragon-fly.

                      Edmund Blunden

THE WELCOME

He'd scarcely come from leave and London,
Still was carrying a leather case,
When he surprised Headquarters pillbox
And sat down sweating in the filthy place.

He was a tall, lean, pale-looked creature,
With nerves that seldom ceased to wince;
Past war had long prayed on his nature,
And war had doubled in horror since.

There was a lull, the adjutant even
Came to my hole : 'You cheerful sinner,
If nothing happens till half-past seven,
Come over then, we're going to have dinner'.

Back he went with his fierce red head;
We were sourly canvassing his jauntiness, when
Something happened at headquarters pillbox.
'Don't go there', cried one of my men.

The shell had struck right into the doorway,
The smoke lazily floated away;
There were six men in that concrete doorway,
Now a black muckheap blocked the way.

Inside, one who had scarcely shaken
The air of England out of his lungs
Was alive, and sane; it shall be spoken
While any of those who were there have tongues.

Edmund Blunden

JANUARY FULL MOON, YPRES

Vantaged snow on the grey pilasters
Gleams to the sight so wan and ghostly;
The wolfish shadows in the eerie places
   Sprawl in the mist-light.

Sharp-fanged searches the frost, and shackles
The sleeping water in broken cellars,
And calm and fierce the witch-moon watches,
   Curious of evil.

Flares from the horse-shoe of trenches beckon,
Momently soaring and sinking, and often
Peer through the naked fire-swept windows
   Mocking the fallen.

Quiet, uneasily quiet—the guns hushed,
Scarcely a rifle-shot cracks through the salient,
Only the Cloth Hall sentry's challenge
   To someone crunching through the frozen snows.
                   Edmund Blunden

CONCERT PARTY – BUSSEBOOM

The stage was set, the house was packed,
   The famous troop began;
Our laughter thundered, act by act;
   Time light as sunbeams ran.

Dance sprang and spun and neared and fled,
   Jest chirped at gayest pitch,
Rhythm dazzled, action sped
   Most comically rich.

With generals and lame privates both
   Such charms worked wonders, till
The show was over : lagging loth
   We faced the sunset chill;

And standing on the sandy way,
   With the cracked church peering past,
We heard another matinée,
   We heard the maniac blast

Of barrage south by Saint Eloi,
   And the red lights flaming there
Called madness : Come, my bonny boy,
   And dance to the latest air.

To this new concert, white we stood;
   Cold certainty held our breath;
While men in the tunnels below Larch Wood
   Were kicking men to death.

                    Edmund Blunden

BREAK OF DAY IN THE TRENCHES

The darkness crumbles away –
It is the same old druid Time as ever.
Only a live thing leaps my hand –
A queer sardonic rat –
As I pull the parapet's poppy
To stick behind my ear.
Droll rat, they would shoot you if they knew
Your cosmopolitan sympathies.
(And God knows what antipathies).
Now you have touched this English hand
You will do the same to a German –
Soon, no doubt, if it be your pleasure
To cross the sleeping green between.
It seems you inwardly grin as you pass
Strong eyes, fine limbs, haughty athletes
Less chanced than you for life,
Bonds to the whims of murder,
Sprawled in the bowels of the earth,
The torn fields of France.
What do you see in our eyes
At the shrieking iron and flame
Hurled through still heavens?
What quaver – what heart aghast?
Poppies whose roots are in man's veins
Drop, and are ever dropping;
But mine in my ear is safe,
Just a little white with the dust.

Isaac Rosenberg

RETURNING, WE HEAR THE LARKS

Sombre the night is :
And, though we have our lives, we know
What sinister threat lurks there.

Dragging these anguished limbs, we only know
This poison-blasted track opens on our camp –
On a little safe sleep.

But hark ! Joy – joy – strange joy.
Lo ! Heights of night ringing with unseen larks :
Music showering on our upturned listening faces.

Death could drop from the dark
As easily as song –
But song only dropped,
Like a blind man's dreams on the sand
By dangerous tides;
Like a girl's dark hair, for she dreams no ruin lies there,
Or her kisses where a serpent hides.

Isaac Rosenberg

DEAD MAN'S DUMP

The plunging limbers over the shattered track
Racketed with their rusty freight,
Stuck out like many crowns of thorns,
And the rusty stakes like sceptres old
To stay the flood of brutish men
Upon our brothers dear.

The wheels lurched over sprawled dead
But pained them not, though their bones crunched;
Their shut mouths made no moan.
They lie there huddled, friend and foeman,
Man born of man, and born of woman;
And shells go crying over them
From night till night and now.

Earth has waited for them,
All the time of their growth
Fretting for their decay :
Now she has them at last !
In the strength of their strength
Suspended – stopped and held.

What fierce imaginings their dark souls lit?
Earth ! Have they gone into you?
Somewhere they must have gone,
And flung on your hard back
Is their souls' sack,
Emptied of God-ancestralled essences.
Who hurled them out? Who hurled?

None saw their spirits' shadows shake the grass,
Or stood aside for the half used life to pass
Out of those doomed nostrils and the doomed mouth,
When the swift iron burning bee
Drained the wild honey of their youth.

What of us who, flung on the shrieking pyre,
Walk, our usual thoughts untouched,
Our lucky limbs as on ichor fed,
Immortal seeming ever?
Perhaps when the flames beat loud on us,
A fear may choke in our veins
And the startled blood may stop.

The air is loud with death,
The dark air spurts with fire,
The explosions ceaseless are.
Timelessly now, some minutes past,
These dead strode time with vigorous life,
Till the shrapnel called 'An end !'
But not to all. In bleeding pangs
Some borne on stretchers dreamed of home,
Dear things, war-blotted from their hearts.

A man's brains splattered on
A stretcher-bearer's face:
His shook shoulders slipped their load,
But when they bent to look again
The drowning soul was sunk too deep
For human tenderness.

They left this dead with the older dead,
Stretched at the cross roads.

Burnt black by strange decay
Their sinister faces lie,
The lid over each eye;
The grass and coloured clay
More motion have than they,
Joined to the great sunk silences.

Here is one not long dead.
His dark hearing caught our far wheels,
And the choked soul stretched weak hands
To reach the living world the far wheels said;
The blood-dazed intelligence beating for light,
Crying through the suspense of the far-torturing wheels
Swift for the end to break
Or the wheels to break,
Cried as the tide of the world broke over his sight,
'Will they come? Will they ever come?'
Even as the mixed hoofs of the mules,
The quivering-bellied mules,
And the rushing wheels all mixed
With his tortured upturned sight.

So we crashed round the bend,
We heard his weak scream,
We heard his very last sound,
And our wheels grazed his dead face.

Isaac Rosenberg

BOMBARDMENT

Four days the earth was rent and torn
By bursting steel,
The houses fell about us;
Three nights we dared not sleep,
Sweating, and listening for the imminent crash
Which meant our death.

The fourth night every man,
Nerve-tortured, racked to exhaustion,
Slept, muttering and twitching,
While the shells crashed overhead.

The fifth day there came a hush;
We left our holes
And looked above the wreckage of the earth
To where the white clouds moved in silent lines
Across the untroubled blue.

Richard Aldington

MY COMPANY
Foule! Ton âme entière est debout dans mon corps.
(Jules Romains)

1

You became
in many acts and quiet observances
a body and a soul, entire.

I cannot tell
what time your life became mine :
perhaps when one summer night
we halted on the roadside
in the starlight only,
and you sang your sad home-songs
dirges which I standing outside you
coldly condemned.

Perhaps, one night, descending cold
when rum was mighty acceptable,
and my doling gave birth to sensual gratitude.

And then our fights : we've fought together
compact, unanimous;
and I have felt the pride of leadership.

In many acts and quiet observances
you absorbed me :
Until one day I stood eminent
and you saw gather'd round me
uplooking
and about you a radiance that seemed to beat
with variant glow and to give
grace to our unity.

But, God ! I know that I'll stand
someday in the loneliest wilderness,
someday my heart will cry
for the soul that has been, but that now
is scatter'd with the winds,
deceased and devoid.

I know that I'll wander with a cry :
'O beautiful men, O men I loved
O whither are you gone, my company?'

2

My men go wearily
with their monstrous burdens.
They bear wooden planks
and iron sheeting
through the area of death. ⟨

When a flare curves through the sky
They rest immobile.

Then on again,
Sweating and blaspheming –
'Oh, bloody Christ !'

My men, my modern Christs,
your bloody agony confronts the world.

3

A man of mine
  lies on the wire.
It is death to fetch his soulless corpse.

A man of mine
  lies on the wire;
And he will rot
and first his lips
the worms will eat.
It is not thus I would have him kiss'd,
but with the warm passionate lips
of his comrade here.

4

I can assume
a giant attitude and godlike mood,
and then detachedly regard
all riots, conflicts and collisions.

The men I've lived with
lurch suddenly into a far perspective :
They distantly gather like a dark cloud of birds
in the autumn sky.

Urged by some unanimous
volition or fate,
Clouds clash in opposition :
The sky quivers, the dead descend;
earth yawns.

They are all of one species.

From my giant attitude,
in godlike mood,
I laugh till space is filled
with hellish merriment.

Then again I assume
my human docility,
bow my head
and share their doom.

    Herbert Read

Just before he left England for the last time on 31 August 1918, Owen was planning a volume of poetry that he never lived to publish, but which he thought of as a kind of propaganda. He scribbled a Preface for it, which began:

> This book is not about heroes. English poetry is not yet fit to speak of them.
> Nor is it about deeds, or lands, nor anything about glory, honour, might, majesty, dominion, or power, except War.
> Above all I am not concerned with Poetry.
> My subject is War, and the pity of War.
> The Poetry is in the pity.
> Yet these elegies are to this generation in no sense consolatory. They may be to the next. All a poet can do today is warn. That is why the true Poets must be truthful.

Owen's best and most typical poetry is in harmony with this Preface. He stresses the tragic waste of war, and so his characteristic attitude is of compassion rather than anger. He fills us with a sense of pity for the dead who died such agonizing and undignified deaths. He makes us painfully aware of all the good that these young men, British and German, could have achieved if only they had lived.

The essential point that Owen has to make is forcibly expressed in 'Insensibility' and 'Strange Meeting'. The first poem begins with a curious half-irony. Owen begins:

> Happy are men who yet before they are killed
> Can let their veins run cold.

He can half forgive men who are insensible to others' misfortunes provided that they are front-line troops about to die, but even then he can only half-forgive them, since to him callous indifference is the worst of sins. He continues to half-forgive old troops at home on leave or new troops only just recruited if *they* forget the men who are actually enduring horror in the front line; but the poem ends with a crescendo of condemnation:

Cursed are dullards whom no cannon stuns,
That they should be as stones.

There was nothing selfish or cowardly about such a poem; Owen did not tell us what will happen 'if "I" should die' but tell us what happened when others died. Pity, in Owen's sense of the word, was not self-pity; it was a positive virtue like that which Macbeth grudgingly admired when he visualized:

Pity, like a naked new-born babe
Striding the blast.

This emotion was as unselfish and as noble as the genuine pity that Byron felt for those who died at Waterloo:

And Ardennes waves above them her green leaves,
Dewy with Nature's teardrops as they pass,
Grieving, if aught inanimate e'er grieves,
Over the unreturning brave.

For Owen pitied others, not himself; his revisions of his poems gradually got rid of all mention of himself; and so his poems present universal pictures of typical scenes on the Western Front. Owen's best poetry is concerned with the plight of individuals only when they are typical of doomed soldiers as a whole, and so the men whose deaths he regrets in poems such as 'Futility' are not identified in the way that Sassoon defines specific casualties:

He was a young man with a meagre wife
And two small children in a Midland town.

Two types of tension give a cutting edge to Owen's best poetry. He cannot quite make up his mind whether God exists and whether pacifism is the only answer to the problem of war. So he carries on an internal debate on these two problems just below the surface of his meaning; the consequent tension gives a terrible intensity to his poetry.

Just as the view he got of rural poverty when he was helping an Oxfordshire vicar before the war made him doubt conventional Christianity, so his terrible experiences in France made him doubt any form of Christianity. Even 'Exposure', which he wrote soon after he first went to France, admits that 'love of God *seems* dying'; as yet, he has too much traditional respect for God to use a stronger verb than *seems*. 'Anthem for Doomed Youth' also provides evidence of Owen's subconscious debate. Its onomatopaeic lines are well known:

> What passing-bells for these who die as cattle?
>   Only the monstrous anger of the guns,
>   Only the stuttering rifle's rapid rattle
> Can patter out their hasty orisons.

Just below the surface of this poem there is a conflict between words (such as 'bells' and 'orisons') with strong religious associations and the harsh realism of phrases such as 'die as cattle'. 'Apologia Pro Poemate Meo', written in November 1917, still professes a belief in God:

> I, too, saw God through mud –
> The mud that cracked on cheeks when wretches smiled.

But 'Asleep' regards as equally likely a romantic, religious afterlife in which the dead soldier is

> High pillowed on calm pillows of God's making

Or a final death in which

> . . . his thin and sodden head
> Confuses more and more with the low mould.

'Spring Offensive' is similarly uncertain about what happens to the dead when it says:

> Some say God caught them even before they fell.

'Greater Love' expresses doubt as to whether it is possible for a good god to exit when he allows such torturing agonies to continue. It describes the dying as:

> Rolling and rolling there
> Where God seems not to care.

But two later poems reject Christianity more openly: 'Futility' arraigns God in the most direct way for ever allowing Creation to take place:

> Was it for this the clay grew tall?
> O what made fatuous sunbeams toil
> To break earth's sleep at all?

A less well known poem, 'The End', expresses the most serious doubts that Owen ever put into poetry. He asks what will happen on the Last Day:

Shall life renew these bodies? Of a truth
All earth will He annul, all tears assuage?

His pious mother removed the second despairing question mark from these lines when she chose them for his tombstone, but her more pessimistic son ended his poem with a speech by Earth who says:

It is death.
Mine ancient scars shall not be glorified,
Nor my titanic tears, the seas, be dried.

His finest poetry, however, is not that in which he despairs; it is that in which his faith and his doubts quiver in the balance.

A similarly uncertain debate about pacifism is hinted at by his best poetry but rarely expressed directly. 'Exposure' briefly states the case *against* pacifism:

Since we believe not otherwise can kind fires burn:
Nor ever suns smile true on child, or field, or fruit.

But in his letters Owen sometimes puts the case for Christian pacifism with passionate intensity:

Already I have comprehended a light which will never filter into the dogma of any national church: namely that one of Christ's essential commands was, Passivity at any price! Suffer dishonour and disgrace, but never resort to arms. Be bullied, be outraged, be killed; but do not kill . . .

Christ is literally in no man's land. There men often hear his voice. Greater love hath no man than this, that a man lay down his life – for a friend.

Is it spoken in English only and French? I do not believe so.

Thus you see how pure Christianity will not fit in with pure patriotism.

Arguments such as this are stated explicitly in his letters but they are only hinted at below the surface of his poems.

Other poets achieved more occasionally than Owen a note of tragic nobility similar to his. Though it has become usual to regard Sassoon as a negative, destructive poet, better at rousing indignation against warmongers than at rousing pity for dead soldiers, nevertheless one must credit his poetry with wider range and more varied effects. A few of his poems plead for all mankind to show genuine sympathy for the dead, like the dead member of 'A Working Party':

Three hours ago he stumbled up the trench:
Now he will never walk that road again:
He must be carried back, a jolting lump,
Beyond all need of tenderness and care.

Sassoon protests against the illogicality of chance which seems to kill off those with most to lose:

He's young, he hated war! how should he die
When cruel old campaigners win safe through?

Such tragedies impel Sassoon to his desperate protest 'O Jesus, make it stop'.

They impelled other poets, both civilians and soldiers, to similar expressions of pity or protest: for instance, Kipling compares the modern soldier's agony to Christ's agony in Gethsemane, and Edward Thomas stresses that a Gloucestershire farm labourer cannot move a fallen tree because his mate has been killed in France. This simple example typifies all that the men might have accomplished whose lives were wasted in war.

GETHSEMANE
1914–18

The Garden called Gethsemane
In Picardy it was,
And there the people came to see
The English soldiers pass.
We used to pass – we used to pass
Or halt, as it might be,
And ship our masks in case of gas
Beyond Gethsemane.

The Garden called Gethsemane,
It held a pretty lass,
But all the time she talked to me
I prayed my cup might pass.
The officer sat on the chair,
The men lay on the grass,
And all the time we halted there
I prayed my cup might pass.

It didn't pass – it didn't pass –
It didn't pass from me.
I drank it when we met the gas
Beyond Gethsemane !

Rudyard Kipling

ATTACK

At dawn the ridge emerges massed and dun
In the wild purple of the glow'ring sun,
Smouldering through spouts of drifting smoke that shroud
The menacing scarred slope; and, one by one,
Tanks creep and topple forward to the wire.
The barrage roars and lifts. Then, clumsily bowed
With bombs and guns and shovels and battle-gear,
Men jostle and climb to meet the bristling fire.
Lines of grey, muttering faces, masked with fear,
They leave their trenches, going over the top,
While time ticks blank and busy on their wrists,
And hope, with furtive eyes and grappling fists,
Flounders in mud. O Jesus, make it stop !

Siegfried Sassoon

A WORKING PARTY

Three hours ago he blundered up the trench,
Sliding and poising, groping with his boots;
Sometimes he tripped and lurched against the the walls
With hands that pawed the sodden bags of chalk.
He couldn't see the man who walked in front;
Only he heard the drum and rattle of feet
Stepping along barred trench boards, often splashing
Wretchedly where the sludge was ankle-deep.

Voices would grunt 'Keep to your right – make way !'
When squeezing past some men from the front-line :
White faces peered, puffing a point of red;
Candles and braziers glinted through the chinks
And curtain-flaps of dug-outs; then the gloom
Swallowed his sense of sight; he stooped and swore
Because a sagging wire had caught his neck.

A flare went up; the shining whiteness spread
And flickered upward, showing nimble rats
And mounds of glimmering sand-bags, bleached with rain;
Then the slow silver moment died in dark.
The wind came posting by with chilly gusts
And buffeting at corners, piping thin
And dreary through the crannies; rifle-shots
Would split and crack and sing along the night,
And shells came calmly through the drizzling air
To burst with hollow bang below the hill.

Three hours ago he stumbled up the trench;
Now he will never walk that road again :.
He must be carried back, a jolting lump
Beyond all need of tenderness and care.

He was a young man with a meagre wife
And two small children in a Midland town;
He showed their photographs to all his mates,
And they considered him a decent chap
Who did his work and hadn't much to say,
And always laughed at other people's jokes
Because he hadn't any of his own.

That night when he was busy at his job
Of piling bags along the parapet,
He thought how slow time went, stamping his feet
And blowing on his fingers, pinched with cold.
He thought of getting back by half-past twelve,
And tot of rum to send him warm to sleep
In draughty dug-out frowsty with the fumes
Of coke, and full of snoring weary men.

He pushed another bag along the top,
Craning his body outward; then a flare
Gave one white glimpse of No Man's Land and wire;
And as he dropped his head the instant split
His startled life with lead, and all went out.

Siegfried Sassoon

THE DEATH-BED

He drowsed and was aware of silence heaped
Round him, unshaken as the steadfast walls;
Aqueous like floating rays of amber light,
Soaring and quivering in the wings of sleep.
Silence and safety; and his mortal shore
Lipped by the inward, moonless waves of death.

Someone was holding water to his mouth.
He swallowed, unresisting; moaned and dropped
Through crimson gloom to darkness; and forgot
The opiate throb and ache that was his wound.
   Water – calm, sliding green above the weir.
   Water – a sky-lit alley for his boat,
   Bird-voiced, and bordered with reflected flowers
   And shaken hues of summer; drifting down,
   He dipped contented oars, and sighed, and slept.

Night, with a gust of wind, was in the ward,
Blowing the curtain to a glimmering curve.
Night. He was blind; he could not see the stars
Glinting among the wraiths of wandering cloud;
Queer blots of colour, purple, scarlet, green,
Flickered and faded in his drowning eyes.

Rain – he could hear it rustling through the dark;
Fragrance and passionless music woven as one;
Warm rain on drooping roses; pattering showers
That soak the woods; not the harsh rain that sweeps
Behind the thunder, but a trickling peace,
Gently and slowly washing life away.

         *   *   *

He stirred, shifting his body; then the pain
Leapt like a prowling beast, and gripped and tore
His groping dreams with grinding claws and fangs.
    But someone was beside him; soon he lay
    Shuddering because that evil thing had passed.
    And death, who'd stepped toward him, paused and stared.

Light many lamps and gather round his bed.
Lend him your eyes, warm blood, and will to live.
Speak to him; rouse him; you may save him yet.
He's young; he hated War; how should he die
When cruel old campaigners win safe through?

But death replied : 'I choose him'. So he went,
And there was silence in the summer night;
Silence and safety; and the veils of sleep.
Then, far away, the thudding of the guns.

                Siegfried Sassoon

BEFORE THE SUMMER

When our men are marching lightly up and down,
When the pipes are playing through the little town,
I see a thin line swaying through wind and mud and rain
And the broken regiments come back to rest again.

Now the pipes are playing, now the drums are beat,
Now the strong battalions are marching up the street,
But the pipes will not be playing and the bayonets will not shine,
When the regiments I dream of come stumbling down the line.

Between the battered trenches their silent dead will lie
Quiet with grave eyes staring at the summer sky.
There is a mist upon them so that I cannot see
The faces of my friends that walk the little town with me.

Lest we see a worse thing than it is to die,
Live ourselves and see our friends cold beneath the sky,
God grant we too be lying there in wind and mud and rain
Before the broken regiments come stumbling back again.

E. A. Mackintosh

IN MEMORIAM
*Private D. Sutherland killed in action in the German trenches,
16 May 1916, and the others who died.*

So you were David's father,
And he was your only son,
And the new-cut peats are rotting
And the work is left undone,
Because of an old man weeping,
Just an old man in pain,
For David, his son David,
That will not come again.

Oh, the letters he wrote you,
And I can see them still,
Not a word of the fighting
But just the sheep on the hill
And how you should get the crops in
Ere the year get stormier,
And the Boches have got his body,
And I was his officer.

You were only David's father,
But I had fifty sons
When we went up in the evening
Under the arch of the guns,
And we came back at twilight –
O God ! I heard them call
To me for help and pity
That could not help at all.

Oh, never will I forget you,
My men that trusted me,
More my sons than your fathers',
For they could only see
The little helpless babies
And the young men in their pride.
They could not see you dying,
And hold you while you died.

Happy and young and gallant,
They saw their first-born go,
But not the strong limbs broken
And the beautiful men brought low,
The piteous writhing bodies,
They screamed 'Don't leave me, sir',
For they were only your fathers
But I was your officer.

                    E. A. *Mackintosh*

BEAUCOURT REVISITED

I wandered up to Beaucourt; I took the river track,
And saw the lines we lived in before the Boche went back;
But Peace was now in Pottage, the front was far ahead,
The front had journeyed Eastward, and only left the dead.

And I thought, How long we lay there, and watched across the wire,
While the guns roared round the valley, and set the skies afire !
But now there are homes in Hamel and tents in the Vale of Hell,
And a camp at Suicide Corner, where half a regiment fell.

The new troops follow after, and tread the land we won,
To them 'tis so much hillside re-wrested from the Hun;
We only walk with reverence this sullen mile of mud;
The shell-holes hold our history, and half of them our blood.

Here, at the head of Peche Street, 'twas death to show your face;
To me it seemed like magic to linger in the place;
For me how many spirits hung round the Kentish Caves,
But the new men see no spirits – they only see the graves.

I found the half-dug ditches we fashioned for the fight;
We lost a score of men there – young James was killed that night;
I saw the star-shells staring, I heard the bullets hail,
But the new troops pass unheeding – they never heard the tale.

I crossed the blood-red ribbon, that once was No Man's Land,
I saw a misty daybreak and a creeping minute-hand;
And here the lads went over, and there was Harmsworth shot,
And here was William lying – but the new men know them not.

And I said, 'There is still the river, and still the stiff, stark trees :
To treasure here our story, but there are only these';
But under the white wood crosses the dead men answered low,
'The new men know not Beaucourt, but we are here – we know'.

                                                        A. P. Herbert

AS THE TEAM'S HEAD-BRASS

As the team's head-brass flashed out on the turn
The lovers disappeared into the wood.
I sat among the boughs of the fallen elm
That strewed an angle of the fallow, and
Watched the plough narrowing a yellow square
Of charlock. Every time the horses turned
Instead of treading me down, the ploughman leaned
Upon the handles to say or ask a word,
About the weather, next about the war.
Scraping the share he faced towards the wood,
And screwed along the furrow till the brass flashed
Once more.
        The blizzard felled the elm whose crest
I sat in, by a woodpecker's round hole,
The ploughman said. 'When will they take it away?'
'When the war's over. So the talk began –
One minute and an interval of ten,
A minute more and the same interval.
'Have you been out?' 'No'. 'And don't want to, perhaps?'
'If I could only come back again, I should.
I could spare an arm. I shouldn't want to lose
A leg. If I should lose my head, why, so,
I should want nothing more.... Have many gone
From here?' 'Yes'. 'Many lost?' 'Yes: good few.
Only two teams work on the farm this year.
One of my mates is dead. The second day
In France they killed him. It was back in March,
The very night of the blizzard, too. Now if
He had stayed here we should have moved the tree.'
'And I should not have sat here. Everything
Would have been different. For it would have been
Another world.' 'Ay, and a better, though
If we could see all all might seem good.' Then
The lovers came out of the wood again :
The horses started and for the last time
I watched the clouds crumble and topple over
After the ploughshare and the stumbling team.

                                 Edward Thomas

THE DEAD FOXHUNTER

We found the little captain at the head;
    His men lay well aligned.
We touched his hand – stone cold – and he was dead,
    And they, all dead behind,
Had never reached their goal, but they died well;
They charged in line, and in the same line fell.

The well-known rosy colours of his face
    Were almost lost in grey,
We saw that, dying and in hopeless case,
    For others' sake that day
He'd smothered all rebellious groans : in death
His fingers were tight clenched between his teeth.

For those who live uprightly and die true
    Heaven has no bars or locks,
And serves all taste . . . or what's for him to do
    Up there, but hunt the fox?
Angelic choirs? No, Justice must provide
For one who rode straight and in hunting died.

So if Heaven had no Hunt before he came,
    Why, it must find one now :
If any shirk and doubt they know the game,
    There's one to teach them how :
And the whole host of Seraphim complete
Must jog in scarlet to his opening Meet.

                                    Robert Graves

TO HIS LOVE

He's gone, and all our plans
    Are useless indeed.
We'll walk no more on Cotswold
    Where the sheep feed
    Quietly and take no heed.

His body that was so quick
  Is not as you
Knew it, on Severn river
  Under the blue
  Driving our small boat through.

You would not know him now ...
  But still he died
Nobly, so cover him over
  With violets of pride
  Purple from Severn side.

Cover him, cover him soon !
  And with thick-set
Masses of memorial flowers –
  Hide that red wet
  Thing I must somehow forget.

Ivor Gurney

LOST IN FRANCE
Jo's Requiem

He had the ploughman's strength
in the grasp of his hand :
He could see a crow
three miles away,
and the trout beneath the stone.
He could hear the green oats growing,
and the south-west wind making rain.
He could hear the wheel upon the hill
when it left the level road.
He could make a gate, and dig a pit,
And plough as straight as stone can fall.
And he is dead.

Ernest Rhys

TRENCH RAID NEAR HOOGE

At an hour before the rosy-fingered
   Morning should come
To wonder again what meant these sties,
These wailing shots, these glaring eyes,
   These moping mum,

Through the black reached strange long rosy fingers
   All at one aim
Protending, and bending : down they swept,
Successions of similars after leapt
   And bore red flame

To one small ground of the eastern distance,
   And thunderous touched.
East then and west false dawns fan-flashed
And shut, and gaped; false thunders clashed.
   Who stood and watched

Caught piercing horror from the desperate pit
   Which with ten men
Was centre of this. The blood burnt, feeling
The fierce truth there and the last appealing,
   'Us? Us? Again?'

Nor rosy dawn at last appearing
   Through the icy shade
Might mark without trembling the new deforming
Of earth that had seemed past further storming.
   Her fingers played,

One thought, with something of human pity
   On six or seven
Whose looks were hard to understand,
But that they ceased to care what hand
   Lit earth and heaven.

Edmund Blunden

INSENSIBILITY

I

Happy are men who yet before they are killed
Can let their veins run cold.
Whom no compassion fleers
Or makes their feet
Sore on the alleys cobbled with their brothers.
The front line withers,
But they are troops who fade, not flowers
For poets' tearful fooling :
Men, gaps for filling :
Losses, who might have fought
Longer; but no one bothers.

II

And some cease feeling
Even themselves or for themselves.
Dullness best solves
The tease and doubt of shelling,
And Chance's strange arithmetic
Comes simpler than the reckoning of their shilling.
They keep no check on armies' decimation.

III

Happy are these who lose imagination :
They have enough to carry with ammunition.
Their spirit drags no pack,
Their old wounds, save with cold, can not more ache.
Having seen all things red,
Their eyes are rid
Of the hurt of the colour of blood for ever.
The terror's first constriction over,
Their hearts remain small-drawn.
Their senses in some scorching cautery of battle
Now long since ironed,
Can laugh among the dying, unconcerned.

IV

Happy the soldier home, with not a notion
How somewhere, every dawn, some men attack,
And many sighs are drained.
Happy the lad whose mind was never trained :
His days are worth forgetting more than not.
He sings along the march
Which we march taciturn, because of dusk,
The long, forlorn, relentless trend
From larger day to huger night.

V

We wise, who with a thought besmirch
Blood over all our soul,
How should we see our task
But through his blunt and lashless eyes?
Alive, he is not vital overmuch;
Dying, not mortal overmuch;
Nor sad, nor proud,
Nor curious at all.
He cannot tell
Old men's placidity from his.

VI

But cursed are dullards whom no cannon stuns,
That they should be as stones;
Wretched are they, and mean
With paucity that never was simplicity.
By choice they made themselves immune
To pity and whatever mourns in man
Before the last sea and the hapless stars;
Whatever mourns when many leave these shores;
Whatever shares
The eternal reciprocity of tears.

Wilfred Owen

FUTILITY

Move him into the sun –
Gently its touch awoke him once,
At home, whispering of fields unsown.
Always it woke him, even in France,
Until this morning and this snow.
If anything might rouse him now
The kind old sun will know.

Think how it wakes the seeds –
Woke, once, the clays of a cold star.
Are limbs, so dear-achieved, are sides,
Full-nerved – still warm – too hard to stir?
Was it for this the clay grew tall?
O what made fatuous sunbeams toil
To break earth's sleep at all?

Wilfred Owen

STRANGE MEETING

It seemed that out of battle I escaped
Down some profound dull tunnel, long since scooped
Through granites which titanic wars had groined.
Yet also there encumbered sleepers groaned,
Too fast in thought or death to be bestirred.
Then, as I probed them, one sprang up, and stared
With piteous recognition in fixed eyes,
Lifting distressful hands as if to bless.
And by his smile, I knew that sullen hall,
By his dead smile I knew we stood in Hell.
With a thousand pains that vision's face was grained;
Yet no blood reached there from the upper ground,
And no guns thumped, or down the flues made moan.
'Strange friend', I said, 'here is no cause to mourn.'

'None,' said the other, 'save the undone years,
The hopelessness. Whatever hope is yours,
Was my life also; I went hunting wild
After the wildest beauty in the world,
Which lies not calm in eyes, or braided hair,
But mocks the steady running of the hour,
And if it grieves, grieves richlier than here.
For of my glee might many men have laughed,
And of my weeping something had been left,
Which must die now. I mean the truth untold,
The pity of war, the pity war distilled.
Now men will go content with what we spoiled.
Or, discontent, boil bloody, and be spilled.
They will be swift with swiftness of the tigress,
None will break ranks, though nations trek from progress.
Courage was mine, and I had mystery,
Wisdom was mine, and I had mastery;
To miss the march of this retreating world
Into vain citadels that are not walled.
Then, when much blood had clogged their chariot-wheels,
I would go up and wash them from sweet wells,
Even with truths that lie too deep for taint.
I would have poured my spirit without stint
But not through wounds; not on the cess of war.
Foreheads of men have bled where no wounds were.
I am the enemy you killed, my friend.
I knew you in this dark : for so you frowned
Yesterday through me as you jabbed and killed.
I parried; but my hands were loath and cold.
Let us sleep now . . .'

                                   Wilfred Owen

5 Bitter Satire

After the campaigns of 1916 had failed to improve either side's chance of winning the war, very respectable right-wing civilians in Germany, France and England thought that the best plan for all was a negotiated peace. For instance, in November 1916 Lord Lansdowne urged the British cabinet to begin peace negotiations because victory was improbable. But it was too late for such a plan to succeed because in August 1916 the Germans had dismissed their commander-in-chief, Falkenhayn, who served Germany very well in 1915 and 1916; his strategy had been to remain on the defensive in the west while inflicting huge defeats on Russia. He was succeeded by Hindenburg and Ludendorff, who believed that a complete German victory was possible.

In many countries there was an internal struggle; on one side there were civilians such as Lansdowne who wanted to negotiate a peace; on the other side were generals who believed in fighting for victory and who were backed up by their civilian supporters, such as Lloyd George. In each country the party that won was the one that believed in a fight to a finish. Indeed, negotiations proved futile because the Allies would only accept peace if Germany would vacate Belgium and Alsace–Lorraine, and the German generals would never agree to do this until they had been decisively defeated. Any suggested concession seemed huge to one side and trivial to the other. Consequently those who tried to negotiate peace in 1917 – international Socialists, the new Austrian emperor and the Pope – had even less chance of success than the right-wing civilians who tried in 1916.

This feeling of hopelessness that led a distinguished minority to contemplate a negotiated peace led several of the poets to write bitter satires against war, though these were brief explosions of anger, not the long, sustained satires that Dryden or Byron wrote.

During the August and Autumn of 1916 Siegfried Sassoon was in Britain on sick leave. He was busy revising the poems that were to appear in *The Old Huntsman* (1917), but he was also busy discussing the ethical problem of the war with Philip Morrell, a Liberal M.P., and his brilliant wife, Lady Ottoline Morrell. They were trying hard to convert a majority of M.P.s to the idea that a negotiated peace was the best solution to Britain's problem. They did not convert many M.P.s but they made a profound impression on Sassoon. In June 1917 when he was again invalided home, he felt a more desperate desire to publicize their ideas and to protest against the way the war was being fought. He was appalled to realize how few yards were gained, and how may thousands of lives were lost, in frontal attacks such as the Somme Offensive. In despair he flung the ribbon of his Military Cross into the Mersey and posted an anti-war protest to his commanding officer so that an M.P. who wanted a negotiated peace, and was being prompted by the pacifist Bertrand Russell, could quote this in the House of Commons as coming from a distinguished officer and poet. Soon afterwards, at Craiglockhart, Sassoon wrote or completed the poems that were to be published in *Counter-Attack* (1918). Many of them were protest poems indignantly implying that the war was being needlessly prolonged by politicians and generals who could have stopped it.

Another impetus that drove front-line soldiers to write satire was the feeling that they belonged to a different race from civilians, especially those who were rich and old. Soldiers were indignant because the old and rich were making a handsome profit out of the war and did not share the soldiers' terrible discomforts and dangers, yet had the effrontery to conceal their selfishness behind a front of self-righteous flag-wagging. In 'Blighters' Sassoon directs this sort of indignation against the vulgar jingoism of a music-hall show and the shallow applause of the civilian audience. In 'Arm-chair' Osbert Sitwell directs a similar type of satire against old men of seventy who cling to vital posts that they are incompetent to hold. In the same mood Owen condemns the old; in his poem 'The Parable of the Old Men and the Young' he envisages Abram as killing Isaac despite God's command to sacrifice a ram instead:

> But the old man would not so, but slew his son,
> And half the seed of Europe, one by one.

This indignant mood that led these soldier poets to satirize civilians is revealed in a letter which Owen wrote to his mother from Scarborough in July 1918:

> This morning at 8.20 we heard a boat torpedoed in the bay, about a mile out. I wish the Boche would have the pluck to come right in and make a clean sweep of the pleasure boats, and the promenaders

on the Spa, and all the stinking Leeds and Bradford war-profiteers now reading *John Bull* on Scarborough Sands.

The soldier poets were desperately keen to mock the false ideas about fighting and dying that were held by civilians. As early as July 1915 Sorley felt the gulf widen between the soldiers and civilians, and in a letter he made fun of civilians' unrealistic notions of soldiering:

I hate the growing tendency to think that every man drops overboard his individuality between Folkestone and Boulogne, and becomes on landing either 'Tommy', with a character like a nice big fighting pet bear and an incurable yearning and whining for mouthorgans and cheap cigarettes, or the Young Officer with a face like a hero and a silly habit of giggling in the face of death.

This exasperation brought Sorley close to the mood that Sassoon was to express a year or two later when he was eager to stress the ugly and shocking aspects of technological warfare in order to show the civilians that war was not as they imagined it. Sassoon's poem 'How to Die' mockingly pretends to accept the popular idea of death in battle, but gives its true purpose away by the sarcastic cheapness of its final phrase: 'Due regard for decent taste'. 'Died of Wounds' and 'Lamentations' are two of the poems in which he caricatures callousness by pretending to share it. Such poems reflect the mood which led Owen, when he was on leave in England and met civilians who talked too glibly about the war, to thrust in front of their eyes photographs of horribly mutilated soldiers.

In certain of his poems Owen imitates Sassoon's type of irony; for instance, in 'The Dead-Beat', he tells how a soldier suddenly drops unconscious and is taken to the casualty-clearing station. The stretcher-bearers label him a 'malingerer', but the poem ends with Owen indignantly mimicking anyone who talks callously about another's death:

Next day I heard the Doc's well-whiskied laugh :
'That scum you sent last night soon died.
               Hooray.'

Another special target for satire was the hypocrisy, self-righteousness and insincerity of the Church. Sassoon's poem 'They' guys the unrealistic Bishop who is delighted with the ways in which war ennobles soldiers:

> 'We're none of us the same', the boys reply.
> 'For George lost both his legs; and Bill's stone blind;
> 'Poor Jim's shot through the lungs and like to die . . .'

In 'At a Calvary near the Ancre' Owen also attacks the militarist chaplains:

> Near Golgotha strolls many a priest,
>   And in their faces there is pride
> That they were flesh-marked by the Beast
>   By whom the gentle Christ's denied.

Owen, who as a patient at Craiglockhart had seen Sassoon's angriest poems before they were published, is here imitating Sassoon's mood and techniques.

Of course, it was not only the soldier-poets who felt bitter. Skilled civilian poets such as Chesterton and Kipling attacked the selfishness and incompetence of the politicians who mismanaged such enterprises as the Mesopotamia campaign. Since Kipling had written imperialist poetry before 1914 he might have been expected to write crudely patriotic poetry now; instead he wrote surprisingly bitter poetry, especially after his only son, a lieutenant in the Irish Guards, was killed in action at Loos.

The methods of the satirical poet were to make far greater use of colloquialisms than poets had ever done since the days of Shakespeare and Donne. Sassoon's verse-forms and rhythms remained traditional; it was his colloquial diction and conversational tones that were startlingly new. Another important satirical technique was to imitate the private language and conventional euphemisms of the big-wigs whom the satirical poets were attacking. Sassoon, especially, mocks the exact words of those whose false attitudes he dramatizes. At other times he is content to use invective, and to write a short poem that makes one simple point with devastating clarity in the way that an effective poster or political cartoon does. Such poetry lacks subtlety, whether or not it uses irony, and it makes a crude assault on the reader's feelings, but its virtues are its burning sincerity and its savage indignation.

One of the usual weapons of satirical poetry, such as Sassoon's, is irony. At its most obvious, this consists of saying the opposite of what one means; for instance, if someone treads on your toe, you might exclaim, 'How gracefully you tread!' Such irony is often called sarcasm when it is crude or bad-tempered.

But poets often use more subtle types of irony. One is to use as a term of abuse (or as a *snarl-word*) a word that is normally used as a term of praise (or as a *purr-word*). For instance, a poet might use the word 'law-abiding', apparently a term of praise, to suggest that some-one kept the letter, but not the spirit, of the law. Another subtle type, much used by Sassoon, is to pretend to agree with arguments, but to present them in so exaggerated or unintelligent a way that they seem ridiculous or hateful to his readers. All these different examples of irony contain an element of incongruity, in that what the poet writes does not fit in with his apparent mood and so jars on the reader. There is a neat contrast between what the poet seems to say, and the effect that he intends to have on his reader.

ELEGY IN A COUNTRY CHURCHYARD

The men that worked for England
They have their graves at home :
And bees and birds of England
About the cross can roam.

But they that fought for England,
Following a falling star,
Alas, alas for England
They have their graves afar.

And they that rule in England,
In stately conclave met,
Alas, alas for England
They have no graves as yet.

G. K. Chesterton

MESOPOTAMIA
(1917)

They shall not return to us, the resolute, the young,
    The eager and whole-hearted whom we gave :
But the men who left them thriftily to die in their own dung,
    Shall they come with years and honour to the grave?

They shall not return to us, the strong men coldly slain
    In sight of help denied from day to day :
But the men who edged their agonies and chid them in their pain,
    Are they too strong and wise to put away?

Our dead shall not return to us while Day and Night divide –
    Never while the bars of sunset hold.
But the idle-minded overlings who quibbled while they died,
    Shall they thrust for high employments as of old?

Shall we only threaten and be angry for an hour?
    When the storm is ended shall we find
How softly but how swiftly they have sidled back to power
    By the favour and contrivance of their kind?

Even while they soothe us, while they promise large amends,
    Even while they make a show of fear,
Do they call upon their debtors, and take counsel with their friends,
    To confirm and re-establish each career?

Their lives cannot repay us – their death could not undo –
    The shame that they have laid upon our race.
But the slothfulness that wasted and the arrogance that slew,
    Shall we leave it unabated in its place?

                                        Rudyard Kipling

EPITAPHS OF THE WAR 1914–18

BATTERIES OUT OF AMMUNITION

If any mourn us in the workshop, say
We died because the shift kept holiday.

A DEAD STATESMAN

I could not dig : I dared not rob :
Therefore I lied to please the mob.
Now all my lies are proved untrue
And I must face the men I slew.
What tale shall serve me here among
Mine angry and defrauded young?

COMMON FORM

If any question why we died,
Tell them, because our fathers lied.
                    Rudyard Kipling

PRAYER FOR THOSE ON THE STAFF

Fighting in mud, we turn to Thee,
    In these dread times of battle, Lord,
To keep us safe, if so may be,
    From shrapnel, snipers, shell, and sword.

But not on us, for we are men
    Of meaner clay, who fight in clay,
But on the Staff, the Upper Ten,
    Depends the issue of the Day.

The staff is working with its brains,
    While we are sitting in the trench;
The Staff the universe ordains
    (Subject to Thee and General French).

God help the staff – especially
    The young ones, many of them sprung
From our high aristocracy;
    Their task is hard, and they are young.

O Lord, who mad'st all things to be,
    And madest some things very good,
Please keep the extra A.D.C.
    From horrid scenes, and sight of blood.

See that his eggs are newly laid,
    Not tinged as some of them – with green;
And let no nasty draughts invade
    The windows of his Limousine.

When he forgets to buy the bread,
    When there are no more minerals,
Preserve his smooth well-oiled head
    From wrath of caustic Generals.

O Lord, who mad'st all things to be,
    And hatest nothing thou has made,
Please keep the extra A.D.C.
    Out of the sun and in the shade.

                        Julian Grenfell

DIED OF WOUNDS

His wet white face and miserable eyes
Brought nurses to him more than groans and sighs :
But hoarse and low and rapid rose and fell
His troubled voice; he did the business well.

The ward grew dark; but he was still complaining
And calling out for 'Dickie'. 'Curse the Wood !
It's time to go. O Christ, and what's the good?
We'll never take it, and it's always raining.'

I wondered where he'd been; then heard him shout,
'They snipe like hell ! O Dickie, don't go out' . . .
I fell asleep . . . Next morning he was dead;
And some Slight Wound lay smiling on the bed.

Siegfried Sassoon

LAMENTATIONS

I found him in the guard-room at the Base.
From the blind darkness I had heard his crying
And blundered in. With puzzled, patient face
A sergeant watched him; it was no good trying
To stop it; for he howled and beat his chest.
And, all because his brother had gone west,
Raved at the bleeding war; his rampant grief
Moaned, shouted, sobbed, and choked, while he was kneeling
Half-naked on the floor. In my belief
Such men have lost all patriotic feeling.

Siegfried Sassoon

HOW TO DIE

Dark clouds are smouldering into red
    While down the craters morning burns.
The dying soldier shifts his head
    To watch the glory that returns;
He lifts his fingers toward the skies
    Where holy brightness breaks in flame;
Radiance reflected in his eyes,
    And on his lips a whispered name.

You'd think, to hear some people talk,
    That lads go west with sobs and curses,
And sullen faces white as chalk,
    Hankering for wreaths and tombs and hearses.
But they've been taught the way to do it
    Like Christian soldiers; not with haste
And shuddering groans; but passing through it
    With due regard for decent taste.

Siegfried Sassoon

DOES IT MATTER?

Does it matter? – losing your legs? . . .
For people will always be kind,
And you need not show that you mind
When the others come in after hunting
To gobble their muffins and eggs.

Does it matter? – losing your sight? . . .
There's such splendid work for the blind;
And people will always be kind,
As you sit on the terrace remembering
And turning your face to the light.

Do they matter? – those dreams from the pit? . . .
You can drink and forget and be glad,
And people won't say that you're mad,
For they'll know you've fought for your country
And no one will worry a bit.

Siegfried Sassoon

'BLIGHTERS'

The House is crammed : tier beyond tier they grin
And cackle at the Show, while prancing ranks
Of harlots shrill the chorus, drunk with din;
'We're sure the Kaiser loves our dear old Tanks !'

I'd like to see a Tank come down the stalls,
Lurching to rag-time tunes, or 'Home, sweet Home',
And there'd be no more jokes in Music-halls
To mock the riddled corpses round Bapaume.

Siegfried Sassoon

TO ANY DEAD OFFICER

Well, how are things in Heaven? I wish you'd say,
  Because I'd like to know that you're all right.
Tell me, have you found everlasting day,
  Or been sucked in by everlasting night?
For when I shut my eyes your face shows plain;
  I hear you make some cheery old remark –
I can rebuild you in my brain,
  Though you've gone out patrolling in the dark.

You hated tours of trenches; you were proud
  Of nothing more than having good years to spend;
Longed to get home and join the careless crowd
  Of chaps who work in peace with Time for friend.
That's all washed out now. You're beyond the wire :
  No earthly chance can send you crawling back;
You've finished with machine-gun fire –
  Knocked over in a hopeless dud-attack.

Somehow I always thought you'd get done in,
  Because you were so desperate keen to live :
You were all out to try and save your skin,
  Well knowing how much the world had got to give.
You joked at shells and talked the usual 'shop',
  Stuck to your dirty job and did it fine :

With 'Jesus Christ ! when will it stop?
　　Three years . . . It's hell unless we break their line'.

So when they told me you'd been left for dead
　　I wouldn't believe them, feeling it *must* be true.
Next week the bloody Roll of Honour said
　　'Wounded and missing' – (That's the thing to do
When lads are left in shell-holes dying slow,
　　With nothing but blank sky and wounds that ache,
Moaning for water till they know
　　It's night, and then it's not worth while to wake !)

*　　*　　*

Good-bye, old lad ! Remember me to God,
　　And tell Him that our politicians swear
They won't give in till Prussian Rule's been trod
　　Under the Heel of England . . . Are you there? . . .
Yes . . . and the War won't end for at least two years;
But we've got stacks of men . . . I'm blind with tears,
　　Staring into the dark. Cheerio !
I wish they'd killed you in a decent show.

Siegfried Sassoon

BASE DETAILS

If I were fierce, and bald, and short of breath,
　　I'd live with scarlet Majors at the Base,
And speed glum heroes up the line to death.
　　You'd see me with my puffy petulant face
Guzzling and gulping in the best hotel,
　　Reading the Roll of Honour. 'Poor young chap',
I'd say – 'I used to know his father well :
　　Yes, we've lost heavily in this last scrap.'
And when the war is done and youth stone dead,
I'd toddle safely home and die – in bed.

Siegfried Sassoon

THE GENERAL

'Good-morning; good-morning !' the General said
When we met him last week on our way to the line.
Now the soldiers he smiled at are most of 'em dead,
And we're cursing his staff for incompetent swine.
'He's a cheery old card', grunted Harry to Jack
As they slogged up to Arras with rifle and pack.

*   *   *

But he did for them both by his plan of attack.

Siegfried Sassoon

INSPECTION

'You ! What d'you mean by this?' I rapped.
'You dare come on parade like this?'
'Please, sir, it's–' ' 'Old yer mouth', the sergeant snapped.
'I takes 'is name, sir?' – 'Please, and then dismiss'.
Some days 'confined to camp' he got,
For being 'dirty on parade'.
He told me, afterwards, the damnèd spot
Was blood, his own. 'Well, blood is dirt', I said.
'Blood's dirt' he laughed, looking away
Far off to where his wound had bled
And almost merged for ever into clay.
'The world is washing out its stains', he said.
'It doesn't like our cheeks so red :
Young blood's its great objection.
But when we're duly white-washed, being dead,
The race will bear Field-Marshal God's inspection.'

Wilfred Owen

AT SENLIS ONCE

O how comely it was and how reviving,
When with clay and with death no longer striving
   Down firm roads we came to houses
   With women chattering and green grass thriving.

Now though rains in a cataract descended,
We could glow, with our tribulation ended –
   Count not days, the present only
   Was thought of, how could it ever be expended?

Clad so cleanly, this remnant of poor wretches
Picked up life like the hens in orchard ditches,
   Gazed on the mill-sails, heard the church-bell,
   Found an honest glass all manner of riches.

How they crowded the barn with lusty laughter,
Hailed the pierrots and shook each shadowy rafter,
   Even could ridicule their own sufferings,
   Sang as though nothing but joy came after !

Edmund Blunden

ARM-CHAIR

If I were now of handsome middle-age,
I should not govern yet, but still should hope
To help the prosecution of this war.
I'd talk and eat (though not eat wheaten bread),
I'd send my sons, if old enough, to France,
Or help to do my share in other ways.

All through the long spring evenings, when the sun
Pursued its primrose path toward the hills,
If fine, I'd plant potatoes on the lawn;
If wet, write anxious letters to the Press.
I'd give up wine and spirits, and with pride
Refuse to eat meat more than once a day,

And seek to rob the workers of their beer.
The only way to win a hard-fought war
Is to annoy the people in small ways,
Bully or patronize them, as you will !
I'd teach poor mothers, who have seven sons
– All fighting men of clean and sober life –
How to look after babies and to cook;
Teach them to save their money and invest;
Not to bring children up in luxury
– But do without a nursemaid in the house !

If I were old or only seventy,
Then should I be a great man in his prime.
I should rule army corps; at my command
Men would rise up, salute me, and attack
– And die. Or I might also govern men
By making speeches with my toothless jaws,
Constant in chatter, until men should say,
'One grand old man is still worth half his pay !'
That day, I'd send my grandsons out to France
– And wish I'd got ten other ones to send
(One cannot sacrifice too much, I'd say).
Then would I make a noble, toothless speech,
And all the list'ning Parliament would cheer.
'We cannot and we will not end this war
Till all the younger men with martial mien
Have enter'd capitals; never make peace
Till they are cripples, on one leg, or dead !'
Then would the Bishops go nigh mad with joy,
Cantuar, Ebor, and the other ones,
Be overwhelmed with pious ecstasy
In thanking Him we'd got a Christian,
An Englishman, still worth his salt, to talk.
In every pulpit would they preach and prance;
And our great Church would work, as heretofore,
To bring this poor old nation to its knees.
Then we'd forbid all liberty, and make
Free speech a relic of our impious past;
And when this war is finished, when the world
Is torn and bleeding, cut and bruised to death,
Then I'd pronounce my peace terms – to the poor !

But as it is, I am not ninety yet,
And so must pay my reverence to these men –
These grand old men, who still can see and talk,
Who sacrifice each other's sons each day.
O Lord ! let me be ninety yet, I pray.
Methuselah was quite a youngster when
He died. Now, vainly weeping, we should say :
'Another great man perished in his prime !'
O let me govern, Lord, at ninety-nine !

Osbert Sitwell

JUDAS AND THE PROFITEER

Judas descended to his lower Hell
   To meet his only friend – the profiteer –
Who, looking fat and rubicund and well,
   Regarded him, and then said with a sneer,
'Iscariot, they did you ! Fool ! to sell
   For silver pence the body of God's Son,
Whereas for maiming men with sword and shell
   I gain at least a golden million.'

But Judas answered : 'You deserve your gold;
It's not His body but His soul you've sold !'

Osbert Sitwell

THE LEVELLER

Near Martinpuisch that night of hell
Two men were struck by the same shell,
Together tumbling in one heap
Senseless and limp like slaughtered sheep.

One was a pale eighteen-year-old,
Blue-eyed and thin and not too bold,
Pressed for the war ten years too soon,
The shame and pity of his platoon.

The other came from far-off lands
With bristling chin and whiskered hands,
He had known death and hell before
In Mexico and Ecuador.

Yet in his death this cut-throat wild
Groaned 'Mother ! Mother !' like a child,
While that poor innocent in man's clothes
Died cursing God with brutal oaths.

Old Sergeant Smith, kindest of men,
Wrote out two copies there and then
Of his accustomed funeral speech
To cheer the womenfolk of each : –

'He died a hero's death: and we
His comrades of "A" Company
Deeply regret his death: we shall
All deeply miss so true a pal.'
                    Robert Graves

AFTER THE BATTLE

So they are satisfied with our Brigade,
    And it remains to parcel out the bays !
And we shall have the usual Thanks Parade,
    The beaming General, and the soapy praise.

You will come up in your capricious car
    To find your heroes sulking in the rain,
To tell us how magnificent we are,
    And how you hope we'll do the same again.

And we, who knew your old abusive tongue,
    Who heard you hector us a week before,
We who have bled to boost you up a rung –
    A K.C.B. perhaps, perhaps a Corps –

We who must mourn those spaces in the mess,
    And somehow fill those hollows in the heart,
We do not want your Sermon on Success,
    Your greasy benisons on Being Smart.

We only want to take our wounds away
    To some warm village where the tumult ends,
And drowsing in the sunshine many a day,
    Forget our aches, forget that we had friends.

Weary we are of blood and noise and pain;
    This was a week we shall not soon forget;
And if, indeed, we have to fight again,
    We little wish to think about it yet.

We have done well; we like to hear it said,
    Say it, and then, for God's sake, say no more.
Fight, if you must, fresh battles far ahead,
    But keep them dark behind your chateau door !

                                        A. P. Herbert

FIVE SOULS

FIRST SOUL

I was a peasant of the Polish plain;
I left my plough because the message ran :
Russia, in danger, needed every man
To save her from the Teuton; and was slain.
I gave my life for freedom – This I know
For those who bade me fight had told me so.

SECOND SOUL

I was a Tyrolese, a mountaineer;
I gladly left my mountain home to fight
Against the brutal treacherous Muscovite;
And died in Poland on a Cossack spear.
I gave my life for freedom – This I know
For those who bade me fight had told me so.

THIRD SOUL

I worked in Lyons at my weaver's loom,
When suddenly the Prussian despot hurled
His felon blow at France and at the world;
Then I went forth to Belgium and my doom.
I gave my life for freedom – This I know
For those who bade me fight had told me so.

FOURTH SOUL

I owned a vineyard by the wooded Main,
Until the Fatherland, begirt by foes
Lusting her downfall, called me, and I rose
Swift to the call – and died in far Lorraine.
I gave my life for freedom – This I know
For those who bade me fight had told me so.

FIFTH SOUL

I worked in a great shipyard by the Clyde;
There came a sudden word of wars declared,
Of Belgium, peaceful, helpless, unprepared,
Asking our aid : I joined the ranks, and died.
I gave my life for freedom – This I know
For those who bade me fight had told me so.

W. N. Ewer

The last section of this anthology includes a miscellany of poems that in various ways manage to look at the war from a distance. Of the poems written during the war Hardy's 'In Time of The Breaking of Nations' and several of A. E. Housman's poems regarded the war with the sombre philosophical detachment that was possible only for ageing civilians in an uninvaded country. McRae imagined how the dead lying beneath the poppies of Flanders would call on future generations to sustain the causes for which they died. Sassoon in 'Everyone Sang' voiced the surprised delight and relief with which mankind greeted the Armistice; of course, he thought of the Armistice as a beginning of social reform as well as an end to mass murder. In poems such as Wilfred Gibson's 'A Lament', and Robert Graves's 'Two Fusiliers' the survivors thought about their dead comrades. Robert Service looked back sentimentally to the 'fine boys' who sang in the Tipperary Days, but he has to admit that the soldiers' songs were frank and comic rather than romantic or patriotic.

Others were more bitter. Philip Johnstone, writing 'High Wood' in 1918, anticipated the patter of travel agents and caretakers who would, in future years, give conducted tours of the battlefields to gaping tourists. Sassoon achieved his most eloquent and condensed indignation in 'Memorial Tablet' and 'On Passing the New Menin Gate', two poems written some time after the Armistice and grimly satirizing the inadequate motives of people who built war memorials. Ezra Pound in 'Pour L'Election de son Sepulchre' expressed the disillusion of the 1920s as it looked back on the war. Cecil Day Lewis in a clever parody showed how the poets of 1930-9 tended to look at the First World War through the eyes of Sassoon and Pound.

When in 1939 the Germans recommenced their attempt to bully and intimidate all Europe, it made people look at the war of 1914-18 in a new light. Somehow Hitler's actions made the motives of 1914 Germany seem clearer and made the war of 1914-18 seem more inevitable. It also made the death of all those young men in the earlier war seem all the more tragic, since the Allied politicians of 1918-39 had thrown away what little the soldiers had gained. Herbert Read expresses some of these feelings in 'To a conscript of 1940'.

After 1945 new generations looked at the First World War in a new way. Clifford Dyment in 'The Son' expresses the pity of sons for the fathers they never saw, whose luck 'had been at the bottom of the sea'. But the poetry of Ted Hughes expresses some of the spirit that made books and plays and television programmes about the First World War fashionable in 1964; he began to find it exciting, and too different from the tragedies of Hiroshima and Nagasaki to be recognizable as the same thing.

IN TIME OF 'THE BREAKING OF NATIONS'

Only a man harrowing clods
   In a slow silent walk
With an old horse that stumbles and nods
   Half asleep as they stalk.

Only thin smoke without flame
   From the heaps of couch-grass;
Yet this will go onward the same
   Though Dynasties pass.

Yonder a maid and her wight
   Come whispering by :
War's annals will cloud into night
   Ere their story die.

Thomas Hardy

HERE DEAD LIE WE

Here dead lie we because we did not choose
   To live and shame the land from which we sprung.
Life, to be sure, is nothing much to lose;
   But young men think it is, and we were young.

A. E. Housman

TWO CANADIAN MEMORIALS

I

We giving all gained all.
    Neither lament us nor praise.
Only in all things recall,
    It is Fear, not Death, that slays.

II

From little towns in a far land we came,
    To save our honour and a world aflame.
By little towns in a far land we sleep;
    And trust that world we won for you to keep !

Rudyard Kipling

IN FLANDERS FIELDS

In Flanders fields the poppies blow
Between the crosses, row on row
    That mark our place; and in the sky
    The larks, still bravely singing, fly
Scarce heard amid the guns below.

We are the Dead. Short days ago
We lived, felt dawn, saw sunset glow,
    Loved and were loved, and now we lie
        In Flanders fields.

Take up our quarrel with the foe :
To you from failing hands we throw
    The torch; be yours to hold it high.
    If ye break faith with us who die
We shall not sleep, though poppies grow
        In Flanders fields.

John McCrae

WHEN I WOULD MUSE IN BOYHOOD

When I would muse in boyhood
   The wild green woods among,
And nurse resolves and fancies
   Because the world was young,
It was not foes to conquer,
   Nor sweethearts to be kind,
But it was friends to die for
   That I would seek and find.

I sought them far and found them,
   The sure, the straight, the brave,
The hearts I lost my own to,
   The souls I could not save.
They braced their belts about them,
   They crossed in ships the sea,
They sought and found six feet of ground,
   And there they died for me.

                    A. E. Housman

A LAMENT

We who are left, how shall we look again
Happily on the sun, or feel the rain,
Without remembering how they who went
Ungrudgingly, and spent
Their all for us, loved, too, the sun and rain?

A bird among the rain-wet lilac sings –
But we, how shall we turn to little things
And listen to the birds and winds and streams
Made holy by their dreams,
Nor feel the heart-break in the heart of things?

                    Wilfrid Gibson

TWO FUSILIERS

And have we done with war at last?
Well, we've been lucky devils both,
And there's no need of pledge or oath
To bind our lovely friendship fast,
By firmer stuff
Close bound enough.

By wire and wood and stake we're bound,
By Fribourt and by Festubert,
By whipping rain, by the sun's glare,
By all the misery and loud sound,
By a Spring day,
By Picard clay.

Show me the two so closely bound
As we, by the wet bond of blood,
By friendship blossoming from mud,
By Death : we faced him, and we found
Beauty in Death,
In dead men, breath.

Robert Graves

EVERYONE SANG

Everyone suddenly burst out singing;
And I was filled with such delight
As prisoned birds must find in freedom,
Winging wildly across the white
Orchards and dark-green fields; on – on – and out of
    sight.

Everyone's voice was suddenly lifted;
And beauty came like the setting sun;
My heart was shaken with tears; and horror
Drifted away ... O, but Everyone
Was a bird; and the song was wordless; the singing will
    never be done.

Siegfried Sassoon

THE FARMER REMEMBERS THE SOMME

Will they never fade or pass –
The mud, and the misty figures endlessly coming
In file through the foul morass,
And the grey flood-water lipping the reeds and grass,
And the steel wings drumming?

The hills are bright in the sun :
There's nothing changed or marred in the well-known places;
When work for the day is done
There's talk, and quiet laughter, and gleams of fun
On the old folks' faces.

I have returned to these;
The farm, and kindly Bush, and the young calves lowing;
But all that my mind sees
Is a quaking bog in a mist – stark, snapped trees,
And the dark Somme flowing.

Vance Palmer

TIPPERARY DAYS

Oh, weren't they the fine boys ! You never saw the beat of them,
Singing altogether with their throats bronze-bare;
Fighting-fit and mirth-mad, music in the feet of them,
Swinging on to glory and the wrath out there.
Laughing by and chaffing by, frolic in the smiles of them,
On the road, the white road, all the afternoon;
Strangers in a strange land, miles and miles and miles of them,
Battle-bound and heart-high, and singing this tune :

> It's a long way to **Tipperary**,
> It's a long way to go;
> It's a long way to **Tipperary**,
> And the sweetest girl I know.
> Goodbye, Piccadilly,
> Farewell, Leicester Square:
> It's a long way to **Tipperary**,
> But my heart's right there.

Come Yvonne and Juliette! Come Mimi and cheer for them!
Throw them flowers and kisses as they pass you by.
Aren't they the lovely lads! Haven't you a tear for them,
Going out so gallantly to dare and die?
What is it they're singing so? Some high hymn of Motherland?
Some immortal chanson of their Faith and King?
Marseillaise or Brabançon, anthem of that other land,
Dears, let us remember it, that song they sing :

> *C'est un chemin long 'to Tepararee',*
> *C'est un chemin long, c'est vrai;*
> *C'est un chemin long 'to Tepararee',*
> *Et la belle fille qu'je connais;*
> *Bonjour, Peekadeely!*
> *Au revoir, Lestaire Squaire!*
> *C'est un chemin long 'to Tepararee',*
> *Mais mon coeur 'ees zaire'.*

The gallant old 'Contemptibles'! There isn't much remains of them,
So full of fun and fitness, and a-singing in their pride;
For some are cold as clabber and the corby picks the brains of them,
And some are back in Blighty, and a-wishing they had died.
Ah me! It seems but yesterday, that great, glad sight of them,
Swinging on to battle as the sky grew black and black;
Yet oh, their glee and glory, and the great, grim fight of them!
Just whistle Tipperary and it all comes back :

> *It's a long way to Tipperary,*
> *(Which means 'ome anywhere);*
> *It's a long way to Tipperary*
> *(And the things wot make you care).*
> *Goodbye, Piccadilly,*
> *('Ow I 'opes my folks is well);*
> *It's a long way to Tipperary –*
> *('R! Aint war just 'ell?)*

Robert Service

HIGH WOOD

Ladies and gentlemen, this is High Wood,
Called by the French, Bois des Fourneaux,
The famous spot which in Nineteen-Sixteen,
July, August and September was the scene
Of long and bitterly contested strife,
By reason of its High commanding site.
Observe the effect of shell-fire in the trees
Standing and fallen; here is wire; this trench
For months inhabited, twelve times changed hands;
(They soon fall in), used later as a grave.
It has been said on good authority
That in the fighting for this patch of wood
Were killed somewhere above eight thousand men,
Of whom the greater part were buried here,
This mound on which you stand being . . .
                              Madame, please,
You are requested kindly not to touch
Or take away the Company's property
As souvenirs; you'll find we have on sale
A large variety, all guaranteed.
As I was saying, all is as it **was,**
This is an unknown British officer,
The tunic having lately rotted off.
Please follow me – this way . . .
                    the *path,* sir, *please,*
The ground which was secured at great expense
The Company keeps absolutely untouched,
And in that dug-out (genuine) we provide
Refreshments at a reasonable rate.
You are requested not to leave about
Paper, or ginger-beer bottles, or orange-peel,
There are waste-paper baskets at the gate.

                    Philip Johnstone

MEMORIAL TABLET
(Great War)

Squire nagged and bullied till I went to fight,
(Under Lord Derby's Scheme). I died in hell –
(They called it Passchendaele). My wound was slight,
And I was hobbling back; and then a shell
Burst slick upon the duck-boards : so I fell
Into the bottomless mud, and lost the light.

At sermon-time, while Squire is in his pew,
He gives my gilded name a thoughtful stare;
For, though low down upon the list, I'm there;
'In proud and glorious memory' . . . that's my due.
Two bleeding years I fought in France, for Squire :
I suffered anguish that he's never guessed.
Once I came home on leave : and then went west . . .
What greater glory could a man desire?

Siegfried Sassoon

ON PASSING THE NEW MENIN GATE

Who will remember, passing through this Gate,
The unheroic Dead who fed the guns?
Who shall absolve the foulness of their fate –
Those doomed, conscripted, unvictorious ones?
   Crudely renewed, the Salient holds its own.
   Paid are its dim defenders by this pomp;
   Paid, with a pile of peace-complacent stone,
   The armies who endured that sullen swamp.

Here was the world's worst wound. And here with pride
'Their name liveth for ever' the Gateway claims.
Was ever an immolation so belied
As these intolerably nameless names?
Well might the Dead who struggled in the slime
Rise and deride this sepulchre of crime.

Siegfried Sassoon

TO A CONSCRIPT OF 1940

*Qui n'a pas une fois désespéré de l'honneur, ne sera jamais
un heros*—Georges Bernanos

A soldier passed me in the freshly-fallen snow,
His footsteps muffled, his face unearthly grey;
And my heart gave a sudden leap
As I gazed on a ghost of five-and-twenty years ago.

I shouted Halt ! and my voice had the old accustomed ring
And he obeyed it as it was obeyed
In the shrouded days when I too was one
Of an army of young men marching

Into the unknown. He turned towards me and I said :
'I am one of those who went before you
Five-and-twenty years ago : one of the many who never returned,
Of the many who returned and yet were dead.

We went where you are going, into the rain and the mud;
We fought as you will fight
With death and darkness and despair;
We gave what you will give—our brains and our blood.

We think we gave in vain. The world was not renewed.
There was hope in the homestead and anger in the streets
But the old world was restored and we returned
To the dreary field and workshop, and the immemorial feud

Of rich and poor. Our victory was our defeat.
Power was retained where power had been misused
And youth was left to sweep away
The ashes that the fires had strewn beneath our feet.

But one thing we learned : there is no glory in the deed
Until the soldier wears a badge of tarnish'd braid;
There are heroes who have heard the rally and have seen
The glitter of a garland round their head.

Theirs is the hollow victory. They are deceived.
But you, my brother and my ghost, if you can go
Knowing that there is no reward, no certain use
In all your sacrifice, then honour is reprieved.

To fight without hope is to fight with grace,
The self reconstructed, the false heart repaired.'
Then I turned with a smile, and he answered my salute
As he stood against the fretted hedge, which was like white lace.

Herbert Read

THE SON

I found the letter in a cardboard box,
Unfamous history. I read the words.
The ink was frail and brown, the paper dry
After so many years of being kept.
The letter was a soldier's, from the front –
Conveyed his love and disappointed hope
Of getting leave. *It's cancelled now,* he wrote.
My luck is at the bottom of the sea.

Outside the sun was hot; the world looked bright;
I heard a radio, and someone laughed.
I did not sing, or laugh, or love the sun,
Within the quiet room I thought of him,
My father killed, and all the other men,
Whose luck was at the bottom of the sea.

Clifford Dyment

BAYONET CHARGE

Suddenly he awoke and was running – raw
In raw-seamed hot khaki, his sweat heavy,
Stumbling across a field of clods towards a green hedge
That dazzled with rifle fire, hearing
Bullets smacking the belly out of the air –
He lugged a rifle numb as a smashed arm;
The patriotic tear that had brimmed in his eye
Sweating like molten iron from the centre of his chest –

In bewilderment then he almost stopped –
In what cold clockwork of the stars and the nations
Was he the hand pointing that second? He was running
Like a man who has jumped up in the dark and runs
Listening between his footfalls for the reason
Of his still running, and his foot hung like
Statuary in mid-stride. Then the shot-blasted furrows

Threw up a yellow hare that rolled like a flame
And crawled in a threshing circle, its mouth wide
Open silent, its eyes standing out.
He plunged past with his bayonet towards the green hedge.
King, honour, human dignity, etcetera
Dropped like luxuries in a yelling alarm
To get out of that blue crackling air
His terror's touchy dynamite.

Ted Hughes

SIX YOUNG MEN

The celluloid of a photograph holds them well –
Six young men, familiar to their friends.
Four decades that have faded and ochre-tinged
This photograph have not wrinkled the faces or the hands.
Though their cocked hats are not now fashionable,
Their shoes shine. One imparts an intimate smile,
One chews a grass, one lowers his eyes, bashful,
One is ridiculous with cocky pride –
Six months after this picture they were all dead.

All are trimmed for a Sunday jaunt. I know
That bilberried bank, that thick tree, that black wall,
Which are there yet and not changed. From where these sit
You hear the water of seven streams fall
To the roarer in the bottom and through all
The leafy valley a rumouring of air go.
Pictured here, their expressions listen yet,
And still that valley has not changed its sound
Though their faces are four decades under the ground.

This one was shot in an attack and lay
Calling in the wire, then this one, his best friend,
Went out to bring him in and was shot too;
And this one, the very moment he was warned
From potting at tin-cans in no-man's-land,
Fell back dead with his rifle-sights shot away.
The rest, nobody knows what they came to,
But come to the worst they must have done, and held it
Closer than their hope; all were killed.

Here see a man's photograph,
The locket of a smile, turned overnight
Into the hospital of his mangled last
Agony and hours; see bundled in it
His mightier-than-a-man dead bulk weight :
And on this one place which keeps him alive
(In his Sunday best) see fall war's worst
Thinkable flash and rending, onto his smile
Forty years rotting into soil.

That man's not more alive whom you confront
And shake by the hand, see hale, hear speak aloud,
Than any of these six celluloid smiles are,
Nor prehistoric or fabulous beast more dead;
No thought so vivid as their smoking blood :
To regard this photograph might well dement,
Such contradictory permanent horrors here
Smile from the single exposure and shoulder out
One's own body from its instant and heat.

Ted Hughes

Notes on the Text

MEN WHO MARCH AWAY
This was published in *The Times* on 9 September 1914.

INTO BATTLE
This poem was published in *The Times* on 27 May 1915, just after Grenfell's death.

And who dies fighting has increase (line 8): fighting has made his life more exciting.

Sisters Seven (line 17): the Pleiades, a cluster of seven stars high overhead in the southern sky, which form an easily recognized constellation. The Greeks imagined they were seven sisters.

Orion's Belt and sworded hip (line 18): the Greeks imagined these stars to form a picture of Orion, the hunter, his upraised arm and club, his belt and his sword. Three bright stars in a line form his belt. His sword, faint to the naked eye, contains a giant nebula. Sirius, one of the very brightest stars, is just below the constellation, to the east (or left) of it.

This poem is a sincere expression of the fierce joy which a minority of men find in fighting. It visualizes the soldier as an embodiment of the instinctive powers of nature; it ignores any moral or patriotic purpose that may lead others to fight.

Bernard Bergonzi in *Heroes' Twilight* defends this poem:

> The attitudes expressed in 'Into Battle' seem almost unimaginably remote now; but they came naturally enough to an aristocratic young cavalry officer of great courage, with a passion for sport and a talent for writing verse, who had not wholly discovered the way the war was shaping by the time he died.

Many modern readers cannot agree with Bergonzi; they regard war as so complete a tragedy that they cannot understand how anyone could get the pleasure out of fighting that Grenfell did—and that Sassoon did to begin with, according to Robert Graves's reminiscences. But Grenfell's poem remains valuable as an eloquent statement of a particular point of view, however much the modern reader disapproves of it.

THE SOLDIER

This sonnet assumes that the typical Englishman is a flower-loving countryman. In a letter written soon after Brooke's death, Charles Sorley wrote:

> That last sonnet-sequence of his . . . which has been so praised, I find (with the exception of that beginning 'These hearts were woven of human joys and cares, washed marvellously with sorrow' which is not about himself) overpraised. He is far too obsessed with his own sacrifice, regarding the going to war of himself (and others) as a highly intense, remarkable and sacrificial exploit, whereas it is merely the conduct demanded of him (and others) by the turn of circumstances. It was not that *they* gave up anything of that list he gives in one sonnet: but that the essence of these things had been endangered by circumstances over which he had no control, and he must fight to recapture them. He has clothed his attitude in fine words: but he has taken the sentimental attitude.

FRANCE

Sassoon, who did not actually have experience in the front line till November 1915, wrote several poems in praise of war that were typical of a general attitude when they were written, but which today clash disconcertingly with the bitter poetry that he wrote from 1916 onwards.

AT THE WARS

yaffle (line 28): the laughing cry of the yellow-hammer which seems to say 'Little bit of bread, no cheese'.

THE DEAD (These hearts were woven . . .)

The worst line is that which narrows the relevance of the poem to a leisured class of dilettantes who merely 'touched flowers and furs and cheeks'.

RENDEZVOUS

I shall not fail that rendezvous (line 24): Alan Seeger did not. He was killed on the Somme on 4 July 1916.

THE VOLUNTEER

the oriflamme (line 8): the sacred banner of St Denis, which French Kings displayed on their lances when starting out for war.

TO MY BROTHER

Sassoon's younger brother was killed at Gallipoli on 15 August 1915.

BEFORE ACTION

This was written two days before Hodgson was killed in action on 1 July 1916, the first day of the Battle of the Somme.

FOR THE FALLEN

Although today we associate this poem with Armistic Day ceremonies, it appeared in *The Times* on 21 September 1914. It is written in a form of free verse whose rhythm is a stately imitation of that in which the Authorized Version translates the obviously poetical parts of the Old Testament, e.g.

> Saul and Jonathan were lovely and pleasant in their lives and in their death they were not divided: they were swifter than eagles, they were stronger than lions . . . How are the mighty fallen in the midst of the battle! (II Samuel, i, 23, 25)

Age shall not weary them (line 14): this line echoes Shakespeare's description of Cleopatra: 'Age cannot wither her, nor custom stale/ Her infinite variety'.

EPITAPH ON AN ARMY OF MERCENARIES

In August 1914, the British Expeditionary Force fought well in Belgium, in particular at the First Battle of Ypres, though ultimately it had to retreat. It prevented the Germans from seizing the Channel Ports, and it helped the French to mount their counter-attack on the Marne (September 1914), which prevented the Germans from winning a quick war. A British newspaper described the professional British soldiers who fought at Ypres as 'mercenaries' and this provoked Housman into writing their epitaph. Housman found the newspaper's use of the word 'mercenaries' insulting; so he sets out to convince us that things done for pay can still be noble.

Their shoulders held the sky suspended (line 5): they were like Atlas, the giant in Greek myths who supported the world with his head and hands. This was a punishment inflicted on him by Jupiter when he replaced Saturn as King of the Gods. Atlas was one of Titans who had resisted Jupiter's seizure of power.

RECRUITING

The repetition of 'Lads', and also the use of the ballad metre, suggest that Mackintosh is imitating A. E. Housman's 'A Shropshire Lad'.

EXPOSURE

This poem was written in February 1917, when Owen had only recently reached the front line. It illustrates the typical universality of Owen's poetry in that it describes life in all trenches or any trench rather than one particular one.

Our brains ache (line 1): Owen begins with an ironic echo of the first line of Keats's 'Ode to a Nightingale': 'My heart aches, and a drowsy numbness pains'. This is the first war poem in which Owen used pararhymes (see page 149).

salient (line 3): an outward bulge in a line of trenches. The army which held it would hold on to it stubbornly in hopes of using it as a base for a further attack later on. Since the enemy could fire at it from three sides, its defence was always very costly.

Slowly our ghosts drag home: glimpsing the sunk fires (line 26): one of Owen's problems was that he derived from his reading of Keats's poetry the gift of writing romantic description, but he could not always find an appropriate use for this. Here he uses it effectively for contrast; the soldiers' daydream of a warm fireside at home contrasts with the bitter cold of the Western Front in the grip of winter.

glozed (line 26): shining, bright.

Since we believe not otherwise can kind fires burn (line 31): here Owen puts forward the case for continuing to fight the war. Sometimes his letters home to his mother put forward the opposite case, the pacifist case (see page 78).

nothing happens (lines 5, 15, 20 and 40): there are several levels of meaning. On one level the line is bitter mimicry of the general or journalist who would sum up the events of such a day as 'All quiet on the Western Front'. On another level this is a protest against the callousness of society which classes a day on which some men are killed (and have to be buried at night in the frosty ground) as one in which *nothing* happens. On a third level the line expresses a tragic awareness of the fact that the day has not brought peace any nearer.

COMRADES: AN EPISODE

In *English Poetry of the First World War* Professor John H. Johnston exaggerates Nichols's faults when he accuses the poet of being obsessed with his own emotional reactions and unaware of the external realities of war. 'There is as yet', Johnston alleges, 'no note of protest or horror.'

'Verey' light (line 2): a kind of flare that could be shot from a pistol. It provided bright, but temporary illumination for part of a battlefield.

GOING INTO THE LINE

This poem was written in August 1916, during the Somme offensive.

SPRING OFFENSIVE

The poem begins with a contrast between the natural, lush beauty of the grassy slope where the soldiers have to wait, and the unnatural hail of machine-gun fire to which they are exposed as soon as they attack. As in 'Exposure', Owen uses his gift for romantic description to achieve contrast.

Had blessed with gold their slow boots coming up (line 15): the epithet 'slow' emphasizes the reluctance of the soldiers to leave behind the beauty, comfort and safety of the meadow with its buttercups.

Leapt to swift unseen bullets, or went up (line 34): Owen kept scribbling alterations in his drafts, and he may have intended this line to read – 'Breasted the surf of bullets, or went up . . .'

Some say God caught them even before they fell (line 37): Owen is not sure whether he can still share the Christian belief in a life after death.

John H. Johnston praises this poem as one of the first war poems that tell a story objectively and successfully. This is the form in which Johnston thinks greater poetry could have been written about the war. This poem suggests that had Owen survived the war, he would have written mature narrative poetry about it.

DULCE ET DECORUM EST

This poem was written in August 1917. The quotation from the Roman poet Horace, which Owen wishes to brand as a lie, means: 'It is sweet and proper to die for the fatherland'.

Of gas-shells dropping softly behind (line 8): Owen may have intended this line to read – 'Of tired out-stripped Five-Nines that dropped behind'.

CLEAR WEATHER

Blunden finds a countryman's pleasure in a fine day.

bandogs (line 10): mastiffs or blood hounds.

An Albatross (line 15): a German biplane fighter aircraft. Also ('and') there is a second plane (line 16), 'one of our own'.

JANUARY FULL MOON, YPRES

Blunden (the countryman who would normally admire the beauty of the winter moonlight) here finds it wolfish and eerie as it illuminates the ruins of Ypres. He thinks of the moon as an evil spectre, haunting the ruined landscape, and not as a romantic goddess. But there is bizarre beauty in these moonlit horrors.

Ypres: Ypres had been an important town for weaving cloth in the late Middle Ages. It contained many beautiful medieval buildings such as the Cloth Hall. It was the scene of bitter fighting throughout the war and of terrible British losses. In the First Battle of Ypres (1914) the British stopped the advance of larger German forces towards the Channel ports. In the Second Battle of Ypres (1915) the Germans used gas for the first time. In the Third Battle of Ypres (1917) Haig made a large-scale attack towards Passchendaele, but lost huge numbers of troops in gaining a few yards of mud.

BREAK OF DAY IN THE TRENCHES

This poem was composed in 1916. It stresses that even compared with the life of a poppy or a rat, a man's life seems tragically short. The rat's function is to make even a low form of life underline how completely dead the soldiers' corpses are. The poppy is a less sentimental emblem than in McCrae's 'In Flanders Fields'. The poppy's roots grow in what were once the veins of men, and seem to derive their redness from the dead soldiers below them. Poppies do not last long but in Flanders they last longer than men. Sassoon said of the poem, 'Sensuous front-line experience is there, hateful and repellent, unforgettable and inescapable'.

RETURNING, WE HEAR THE LARKS

The incongruous beauty of the larks' song has a powerful effect on soldiers whose life has been starved of beauty and filled instead with ugliness, darkness and danger. The reader is intended to contrast these larks heard in the trenches with Shelley's skylark.

DEAD MAN'S DUMP

Rosenberg wrote to Sir Edward Marsh (editor of *Georgian Poetry*) on 8 May 1917: 'I've written some lines suggested by going out wiring, or rather carrying up the line on limbers and running over dead bodies lying about'. The title impresses on us the callousness of warfare and its brutal indifference to carnage. The 'rusty stakes . . . To stay the flood' (lines 4–5) reminds us of Canute's inability to hold back the sea; such phrases are typical of this poem which is a blend of realism and symbolism.

crowns of thorns (line 3): Rosenberg, like Sassoon and Owen in some moods, thinks of the ordinary soldier on the Western front as having been tortured by the world's rulers and ruling classes in much the same way as Christ was.

Our lucky limbs as on ichor fed (line 34): Greek mythology imagined that 'ichor' was a special sort of blood in the veins of gods.

MY COMPANY

Sir Herbert Read wrote this poem in 1931; it analyses the psychological relationship between an officer and the men he leads. Sir Herbert describes how the officer commanding a company gradually becomes part of its corporate life. But in actual battle he alternately rejects, and returns to, this identification of himself with his men. The epigraph means: 'My men, your corporate soul has entered and engulfed my body'.

GETHSEMANE

On the night before he was crucified Jesus prayed in the garden of Gethsemane. He was in an agony of indecision while he prayed, 'O my father, if it is possible, let this cup pass from me: Nevertheless, not as I will, but as thou will'. While he prayed Peter and John, whom he had told to 'watch' (i.e. to stay awake) and 'pray' had gone to sleep.

Picardy (line 2): the old name for the area of France that includes Arras, Amiens and the valley of the Somme.

ATTACK

Lines of grey, muttering faces, masked with fear (line 9): compared with Owen, Sassoon tends to put more stress on the psychological effects on men of waiting to go over the top, and less on the physical effects of wounds. Sassoon stresses the terrible anxieties that war brings.

A WORKING PARTY

He was a young man with a meagre wife (line 30): Sassoon stresses the ordinariness of the man for whom he invites our pity. The dead soldier is different in every way from the conventional hero of poetry.

BEFORE THE SUMMER

This was written in 1916, just before the Battle of the Somme.

BEAUCOURT REVISITED

Hamel (line 7): Beaumont Hamel was at the northern end of the sector which the British attacked with tragic loss of life, and disappointingly small gain of ground, from 1 July 1916 onwards.

the river (line 25): the Somme.

TRENCH RAID NEAR HOOGE

At an hour before the rosy-fingered/Morning should come (lines 1 and 2): with a strange semi-irony Blunden begins with the sort of description of dawn that Homer wrote and that his imitators, such as Thomas Gray, have copied in their rather artificial poetry. There is a terrible contrast between this decorous literary dawn and the grim fire of the bombardment that preceded it. War is shown as destroying the harmony of the world of nature—this one detail, that the battle begins one hour *before* the dawn, is typical of a general unnaturalness.

INSENSIBILITY

It is undated, but Owen probably wrote it at Scarborough very late in 1917. It condemns all who lost human sympathy and turn from innocence to callousness. Owen cannot forgive civilians for lacking pity for those who die in wars. He begins the poem by grudgingly allowing soldiers who are going to be killed themselves to lose some sense of pity for their comrades. But since Owen regards insensibility as the worst of evils, there is complicated irony in the word 'happy' with which the poem begins.

fleers (line 3): mocks.

But cursed are dullards (line 50): the poem ends with a burning protest against civilians who are immune to pity.

FUTILITY

fields unsown (line 3): they are symbolic of the promise of youth that the dead soldier has not been able to fulfil; also, more literally, the dead man worked on a farm.

O what made fatuous sunbeams toil (line 13): nothing could express a deeper disillusion than these two last lines. Owen protests against the power of evil, and arraigns the Creator. In a century which has given far too much power to governments and seen far too many wars, Owen asserts that the individual matters; and so he asks why such tragedies as this man's death should occur.

STRANGE MEETING

The opening incident, in which Owen finds a dead German in a tunnel excavated below the German line, may have been suggested to him by the incident recounted in Sassoon's 'The Rear-Guard'.

In the early lines Owen uses a new type of assonance (e.g. 'granites/titanic'; 'distressful/bless') to suggest that the noises of battle penetrate the tunnel of his dream.

Then, as I probed them, one sprang up, and stared: Owen is writing an epitaph for The Unknown Soldier, for every dead soldier.

titanic (line 3): the Titans were giants who were conquered and supplanted by the later race of gods when Zeus dethroned Saturn.

braided (line 19): bound with ribbon.

They will be swift with swiftness of the tigress (line 28): Owen forecasts the economic crises of the 1920s, then the rise of the totalitarian states and the march to a second world war. Owen sees the role of the poet as a sort of social Cassandra. It is grimly ironic, in view of the later rise of Hitler, that Owen puts these prophetic lines into the mouth of a German.

Even with truths that lie too deep for taint (line 36): this is an ironic echo of the last line of Wordsworth's 'Ode on the Intimations of Immortality': 'Thoughts that do often lie too deep for tears'.

I am the enemy you killed, my friend (line 40): it is a remarkable sign of the greatness of Owen's vision that he could have sympathy for a dead German. Also the dead man, unlike Rupert Brooke, does not regret what he could have enjoyed had he lived longer; instead he regrets how he lost the chances to improve the world. Owen shows that the First World War has changed the whole direction of history for the worse and has done incalculable damage to mankind.

ELEGY IN A COUNTRY CHURCHYARD

The title is, of course, an ironic echo of Thomas Gray's poem. The phrase, 'in stately conclave met' (line 10), is also an ironic echo of *Paradise Lost*, Book I, line 795, which describes how in Hell the chief devils, Satan's inner cabinet—'In close recess and secret conclave sat'.

MESOPOTAMIA

This is a sad poem today because the politicians whom Kipling attacks for having planned the Mesopotamia campaign so badly were mostly able to keep in office after the war.

At different times during the war the British made attacks on various parts of what was then the huge ramshackle Turkish empire. Some of these were disastrous. In 1916 an army under Townshend that invaded Mesopotamia (Iraq) had to surrender at Kut–el–Amara.

PRAYER FOR THOSE ON THE STAFF

This seems to have been the first satirical poem to have been written about the Great War. It is strikingly different from other poems written in 1915 and other poems written by Grenfell.

LAMENTATIONS

In such poems Sassoon caricatures the callous attitudes to death and suffering that he hates. The irony is elaborate, since he *pretends* to adopt the romantic view of dying in war, and the popular romantic idea of what death in battle is like.

HOW TO DIE

It parodies the heroic manner; the irony is revealed by the cheapness of the key phrase ('decent taste') that he uses to express (and so expose) the conventional view.

DOES IT MATTER?

Sassoon mimics civilians who try to console wounded soldiers with silly arguments.

the pit (line 11): the depth of despair.

'BLIGHTERS'

John H. Johnston is unfairly critical of this type of poem, saying 'The anger here is certainly excessive and without a worthy target'.

In January 1917, just before Sassoon returned to France, he was infuriated by a jingoist music hall programme at the Liverpool Hippodrome.

Bapaume (line 8): south of Arras and north-east of Amiens. It was held by the Germans throughout 1916.

BASE DETAILS

Sassoon later described his own technique in this sort of satirical poem as 'composing two or three harsh, peremptory and colloquial stanzas with a knock-out blow in the last line'. Sassoon's poem mimics the typical major's euphemism and clichés as well as his false attitude to war.

INSPECTION

In the few poems that he wrote in a satirical vein, Owen imitated Sassoon's technique of using just the words that soldiers—both privates and officers—would use.

damnèd spot (line 7): when Lady Macbeth walks in her sleep, she rubs her hands, which she imagines to be stained with Duncan's blood, and exclaims, 'Out, damnèd spot'.

But when we're duly white-washed (line 15): soldiers prepare their barracks for an inspection by a Field-Marshal by pointless methods of making them look better, such as white-washing the coal. Similarly warmongering mankind makes young men's cheeks fit for inspection by Field-Marshal God, by emptying them of blood; governments and churches thus equate God with a field-marshal who can easily be deceived.

AT SENLIS ONCE

Senlis is only a few miles north of Paris.

There is irony in the opening lines which echo words spoken by the Chorus in Milton's *Samson Agonistes*:

> O how comely it is and how reviving
> To the spirits of just men long oppressed
> When God into the hands of their deliverer
> Puts invincible might.

Blunden shows how war falsifies all human values. It makes the most humble activities of life become intense pleasures because they are such a relief from the horrors of the front line. It is therefore a tragic disharmony of natural happy life.

ARM-CHAIR

Cantuar, Ebor (line 41): Archbishops of Canterbury and York.

Methuselah (line 58): according to the Old Testament he lived to be 969 years old (Genesis v, 27).

THE LEVELLER

This title is a reference to a poem by John Shirley called 'Death, the Leveller' which stresses that kings die as well as farm labourers.

FIVE SOULS

The five dead soldiers were:

1 A Polish peasant who was persuaded to fight for Russia against Germany and Austria. In 1914 Russia ruled over most of Poland.
2 An Austrian who fought against Russia in Poland.
3 A Frenchman who fought against Germany in Belgium.
4 A German who died fighting against the French in Lorraine, a part of France which the Germans seized in 1870 and were forced to give back in 1919.
5 A Scot who fought against the Germans.

IN TIME OF 'THE BREAKING OF NATIONS'

Jeremiah, li, 20: 'Thou art my battle axe and weapons of war; for with thee I will break in pieces the nations, and with thee will I destroy Kingdoms'.

couch-grass (line 6): a common weed, a coarse grass with creeping white roots. It is known in other parts of England as 'quitch' or 'squitch'.

WHEN I WOULD MUSE IN BOYHOOD

This poem was written in 1922 when Housman was preparing to publish *Last Poems*.

THE FARMER REMEMBERS THE SOMME

The farmer is back in Australia.

TIPPERARY DAYS

The gallant old 'Contemptibles' (line 33): Since the Kaiser had referred slightingly to Britain's 'Contemptible little army', the professional soldiers who fought at Mons, in August 1914, nicknamed themselves 'The Old Contemptibles'.

HIGH WOOD

This bitter poem was written *during* the war.

MEMORIAL TABLET

Passchendaele (line 3): from July to November 1917 the British lost a disastrous number of men in frontal attacks in south-west Belgium in the area of Ypres and Passchendaele. Among the reasons for the failure of the attacks was the incredibly wet weather.

ON PASSING THE NEW MENIN GATE

One of the beautiful old buildings destroyed in Ypres was the medieval gate by which the road to Menin left the town. After the war this was rebuilt as a large memorial to the many British dead who died in the Ypres sector.

TO A CONSCRIPT OF 1940

The epigraph means—He who has never once given up hope will never be a hero.

Sir Herbert Read writes this poem soon after the beginning of the Second World War. In an unusual mood he argues that the bravest soldier is the one who does not really expect war to achieve anything.

ALDINGTON, RICHARD (p. 72)

Born in 1892. He served on the Western Front and was badly gassed. He later wrote an angry anti-war novel 'Death of a Hero'. He has written a number of biographies, such as those of Wellington and Lawrence of Arabia; in some of them he has taken a very unorthodox view of the person whose life he has written. His poetry shows the influence of the Imagists, notably T. E. Hulme and Ezra Pound; he uses vers libre, avoiding orthodox verse rhythms, and he attaches great importance to images which are presented with frank accuracy in language that is free from literary artificiality. He was one of the first to write Imagist poetry about the war. Died in 1962.

ASQUITH, HERBERT (p. 32)

Born in 1881. His father was the Liberal Prime Minister from 1908 to 1916 when he was ousted by Lloyd George because he was thought not to have led the war effort with enough resolution. Herbert Asquith himself was considered one of the leading Georgian poets in the period 1910–14; he and his brother were close personal friends of Rupert Brooke. Some of the poems that he wrote for children, such as 'The Elephant', are still well known. He served on the Western Front in the artillery. Died in 1947.

BINYON, LAURENCE (pp. 36, 41–2)

Born in 1869. He was typical of the older generation of civilian poets who wrote about the war. In 1916 he went to the front line as a Red Cross orderly. After working for forty years in the British Museum, he became Professor of Poetry at Harvard when he retired. Died in 1943.

BLUNDEN, EDMUND (pp. 64–7, 90, 108)

Born in 1896 near Maidstone. He served with The Royal Sussex Regiment, 1915–19; with it he experienced some of the bitterest and bloodiest fighting of the war, especially in the later stages of the Battle of the Somme (1916) and in the Ypres salient (1917). He won the

Military Cross. He was invalided home in March 1918. On leaving the army Blunden sent some of his nature poetry to Siegfried Sassoon, who was then the acknowledged war poet. Sassoon describes in *Siegfried's Journey* how thrilled he was to find a poet writing about a Kentish barn with the vividness he would have liked to achieve himself: 'Here, too, was description of mill-wheel and weir, beautifully exact and affectionately felt, where authentic fishes basked in glades of drowsy sun'. It was as a nature poet, not as a war poet, that Blunden sought a reputation; he seems to have regarded the war as an untypical episode in his life and he published his war poems only as an appendix to his autobiographical prose book, *Undertones of War* (1928). In between the wars he held a series of posts at universities, including Tokyo and Oxford; he also continued as a fluent writer of poems about country life and in traditional styles. In 1966 he was elected Professor of Poetry in the University of Oxford. His war poetry has more variety and equanimity than most; one of its recurrent themes is a study of how the normal harmonies of nature and country life are destroyed by the abnormal ugliness and devastation of war. He makes his points more subtly than Sassoon; he implies the poignant contrast between the war-ravaged countryside of France and the peaceful beauty that it once possessed. He has less sense of moral outrage than Sassoon and Owen felt.

BROOKE, RUPERT (pp. 26, 29)

Born in 1887. He was well known as a poet before 1914; among his best-known poems was 'The Old Vicarage', and 'Grantchester', a fanciful nostalgic poem which he wrote about Cambridge villages while he was travelling in Germany. When in 1912 Edward Marsh edited the first volume of *Georgian Poetry*, which he hoped would herald a new age of poetry showing 'a new strength and beauty', he included 'The Old Vicarage'. In 1914 Brooke joined the Navy and fought in the unsuccessful defence of Antwerp, where the naval brigade fought as though they were soldiers. He wrote his five famous war sonnets at Rugby School during the last months of 1914 when he was home on leave. Since he was a friend of the young Asquiths, 10 Downing Street was another place where he stayed when on leave. He served in the fleet that was attacking the Turkish positions in the Dardanelles, but on 23 April 1915 he died of blood poisoning on a French hospital ship in the Aegean Sea. He was buried on the top of a high hill, on the Greek island of Skyros; among the burial party were

Arthur Asquith (brother of Herbert Asquith, and son of the Prime Minister) and Bernard Freyburg, V.C. (the New Zealander who was later to command the British forces in Crete in 1941).

As Sir Edward Marsh put it:

> Here then, in the island where Theseus was buried, and whence the young Achilles and the young Pyrrhus were called to Troy, Rupert Brooke was buried on Friday, 23 April, the day of Shakespeare and St George.

Brooke willed the posthumous income from his royalties to Lascelles Abercrombie, Wilfred Gibson and Walter de la Mare, who were thus helped to devote their lives to writing poetry.

Critics have formed opposite estimates of Brooke's poetry. For instance, F. R. Leavis wrote:

> His verse exhibits a genuine sensuousness rather like Keats's (though more energetic) and something that is rather like Keats's vulgarity with a Public School accent.

On the other hand Robert Nichols was still insisting in 1943 that:

> Rupert Brooke's sonnets are full of that sensation of being gathered up. They are wonderful works of art and it is sad that they have come to be regarded by many with suspicion.

CHESTERTON, GILBERT KEITH (p. 99)

Born in 1874 in Kensington, he became a student at the Slade School in 1891. Despite showing promise as a draughtsman he soon turned to a literary career and remained a very versatile writer all his life. His best known poems are the long poem 'Lepanto', his short poem 'The Donkey', and the poem in which he describes how

> The rolling English drunkard made the rolling English road.

He wrote successful detective stories in which the sleuth was a Roman Catholic priest, Father Brown, whose Pickwickian simplicity hid his insight until he solved each crime. He wrote witty essays full of paradoxes, and stimulating controversial biographies of writers such as Browning, Chaucer and Dickens. He was an argumentative writer, quick to enter public controversies and quite sure that to joke about topics such as religion could be as serious in purpose as a solemn approach. He looked like a caricature of Harry Secombe caricaturing Mr Pickwick; and Shaw, humorously echoing *Gulliver's Travels*, called him 'The Man-Mountain'. He was always critical of the idea of Evolution and he claimed to attack Capitalism for the exactly opposite reasons to those of the Socialists. In 1922 he became a Roman Catholic and took part in many arguments as an ally of Hilaire Belloc, who condemned a Protestant historian as the

> Remote and ineffectual Don
> That dared attack my Chesterton.

DYMENT, CLIFFORD (p. 124)

Born in Derbyshire in 1914. He has had a great variety of jobs—being, for instance, shop assistant, travelling salesman, clerk, book reviewer, documentary film director, and freelance broadcaster. In 1950 he received the Atlantic Award in Literature. In recent years he has not only continued to publish poetry and to edit editions of the poetry of Matthew Arnold and Thomas Hood, but has produced films for both the BBC and Granada. In *Who's Who* he lists his recreations as 'sampling cheap wines, listening to 78 r.p.m. gramophone records and playing the mouth organ'.

EWER, W. N. (p. 113)

Born in 1885. He has written several books about diplomacy and foreign relations.

GIBSON, WILFRID WILSON (p. 57, 117)

Born in 1878 in Hexham, Northumberland. Although he was not physically strong, he tried hard to serve society, first as a social worker in the East End of London, and then as a private on the Western Front. His poems usually are narrative in form even when they are short; the best known is probably, 'Flannan Isle'. Before the war, in poems such as 'The Ice-Cart', he was one of the first writers to portray commercial and industrial life as it really was; during the war he was similarly one of the first poets to introduce savage realism into his writing. After the war he lived in Gloucestershire to be near his close friend and fellow poet, Lascelles Abercrombie. Both had been friends of Rupert Brooke and both derived enough income from the posthumous sales of Brooke's poems to devote their lives to writing poetry. Gibson won the Hawthornden Prize in 1920. Died in 1962.

GRAVES, ROBERT (pp. 88, 111, 118)

Born in London in 1895. He fought on the Western Front with The Royal Welch Fusiliers for long periods in 1915, 1916 and 1917; during this time he fought at Loos and on the Somme, where he was seriously wounded. He was a close friend of Sassoon (who was in the same regiment) and later of Owen and Nichols. He was incorrectly reported 'Died of wounds' on his twenty-first birthday. He was one of the first war poets to describe the revolting details of war with unflinching realism. He has continued throughout his life to add to his literary reputation—as author of a book of prose reminiscences about the war, *Goodbye to All That*; as author of *I, Claudius* and *Claudius, the God*, two popular books about life at court in ancient Rome; as a poet whose high quality has been more widely recognized since 1945; and as one of the holders—like Edmund Blunden—of the elective post of Professor of Poetry in the University of Oxford (1961–6).

GRENFELL, JULIAN (pp. 25–6, 102)

Born in 1888. He joined the Royal Dragoons as a regular officer in 1910 and enjoyed the life of a cavalry officer in India with its manoeuvres, polo, buck-stalking and pig-sticking. He continued to serve with the same regiment in France, though now the Dragoons were converted to infantrymen in the trenches. He won the D.S.O. for stalking German snipers and killing them at point-blank range. His letters show the same exultation about war as his most famous poems; he was one of the minority who sincerely enjoyed fighting. He was wounded in the head near Ypres and died in hospital at Boulogne on 26 May 1915.

GURNEY, IVOR (pp. 88–9)

He was a Gloucestershire poet and composer of great promise—a pupil of Parry and Vaughan Williams. He fought on the Western Front in the ranks and was so shattered by his experiences that finally he died in a mental hospital (1937). During his last years he was unable to distinguish the past from the present and continued writing war poetry as though the war were still on.

HARDY, THOMAS (pp. 24, 115)

Born near Dorchester in 1840, the son of a stone-mason. After beginning a career as an architect, he became famous as the writer of a series of novels about 'Wessex', his name for Dorset and its neighbouring rural counties. These were published between 1871 and 1896. After that he published very little except poetry, and it caused a literary sensation when a famous novelist began publishing poetry at 58. Some of his poems, however, had been written many years before; indeed Hardy presents the unusual picture of a poet whose best poems were written in his twenties and his seventies. Although he was 74 when the war broke out he wrote several outstanding poems about it. Died at Dorchester in 1928.

HERBERT, A. P. (pp. 86, 112)

Born in 1890 in London. As a lieutenant in the Royal Naval Division he fought both at Gallipoli and on the Somme. He became well known afterwards as a novelist, as a witty contributor to *Punch*, as a writer of libretti for musical comedies such as *Bless the Bride*, and as the Independent M.P. for Oxford University from 1935 to 1949. His private member's bill, finally passed into law as the Matrimonial Causes Act of 1937, secured a major reform in Britain's divorce laws; it was the first British bill to allow divorce on other grounds besides adultery—e.g. cruelty.

HODGSON, WILLIAM NOEL (pp. 34–5)

Born in 1893, the third and youngest son of the Bishop of St Edmundsbury and Ipswich. As soon as he read Brooke's war sonnets he was impelled to enlist. He received a commission in the Devon Regiment, was mentioned in despatches, and won the Military Cross in October 1915. He was killed on 1 July 1916, the first day of the Battle of the Somme. His posthumous collection *Verse and Prose in Peace and War* was very popular when it first appeared, and is still stocked by public libraries.

HOUSMAN, A. E. (pp. 39, 115, 117)

Born in 1859. He failed his final examinations in classics at Oxford, chiefly because he read everything except the set books. So resolutely did he set out to prove himself a scholar, in defiance of this examination result, that he became Professor of Latin at University College, London, and finally at Cambridge. His collections of poetry, *A Shropshire Lad* (1890) and *Last Poems* (1923) made him famous. Died at Trinity College, Cambridge, in 1936.

HUGHES, TED (pp. 125–7)

Born at Mytholmroyd in Yorkshire. His poetry has won high praise. He finds in the soldiers of the First World War similar admirable qualities to those he finds in animals—a positive vitality and a violent power that he finds lacking in modern urban life. He believes in the essential goodness of our powerful instinctive impulses. 'What excites my imagination', he once said, 'is the war between vitality and death.'

JOHNSTONE, PHILIP (p. 121)

'High Wood' was first published in *The Nation* on 16 February 1918.

KIPLING, RUDYARD (pp. 79–80, 100–1, 116)

Born in Bombay in 1865. He was a cousin of Stanley Baldwin, who was Conservative Prime Minister for a few months in 1923 and then from 1924 to 1929 and from 1935 to 1937. Kipling was a copious writer of poetry and novels throughout his life, and was almost the only well-known poet to write poetry in praise of soldiers, especially privates, before 1914. Unlike the Georgian poets, he wrote poetry in which he showed more interest in people than in places, and in which he experimented with a variety of metres and colloquial vocabulary. Because his only son, a lieutenant in the Irish Guards, was killed at Loos, he helped pay for many years for the endowment which made it possible for the Last Post to be sounded every night at the Menin Gate memorial, Ypres. Died in 1936.

MACKINTOSH, E. A. (pp. 45–6, 84–5)

Born in 1893. He joined the Seaforth Highlanders and won the M.C. in France. He was killed in action at Cambrai in October 1917.

MCCRAE, JOHN (p. 116)

Born in Canada in 1872. He was a distinguished doctor who wrote an important book on pathology. He went to Europe in 1914 as a gunner, but was transferred to the medical service and served as a doctor in the front line during the Second Battle of Ypres. His famous poem, 'In Flanders Fields' appeared anonymously in *Punch* on 8 December 1915. He was appointed to take charge of a hospital at Boulogne, but died of pneumonia in January 1918 before he could take up his appointment.

NICHOLS, ROBERT (pp. 27–8, 53–6)

Born in 1893 at Shanklin, Isle of Wight. Before 1914 he was a friend of Brooke and Edward Marsh and also Sassoon; and was thought of as a leading Georgian poet. In October 1914 he was commissioned in the Royal Field Artillery and in 1915 he fought on the Somme, but he was soon invalided out of the army with shell-shock from which he never fully recovered. He tried to write realistic descriptions of battle, but these sometimes lapsed into sentimentality. Even in 1916 he could write:

> What need of comfort has the heroic soul?
> What soldier finds a soldier's grave is chill?

His two volumes of war poetry, *Invocation: War Poems and Others* (1915) and *Ardours and Endurances* (1917), sold well at once, and after he was invalided out of the forces he gave emotional public readings of them to large audiences in Britain and the U.S.A. From 1921 to 1924 he was Professor of English Literature in the University of Tokyo, a post in which he was succeeded by Blunden. Died in 1944.

OWEN, WILFRED (pp. 46–7, 61–3, 91–4, 107)

Born in Oswestry in 1893. From 1911 to 1913 he was a lay assistant to the Vicar of Dunsden, in Oxfordshire, as his parents, who were very religious, hoped he would enter the Anglican priesthood. This upbringing had an obvious influence on his poetry with its Biblical phrases and its broodings over the theological justification of war. From 1913 to 1915 he held posts as a private tutor in France, but in October 1915 he returned to England to enlist, and in June 1916 he was commissioned in the Manchester Regiment. Very early in 1917 he was in the front line on the Somme with the Lancashire Fusiliers. His letters to his mother reveal how shocked he was to discover the horror and muddle of war at the front in wintertime. For instance in no-man's land all water froze, so that men were in simultaneous danger of death from thirst, frostbite and snipers' bullets; they felt 'marooned in a frozen desert'. After being declared a casualty in March and May 1917 he was invalided home with neurasthenia and sent to Craiglockart War Hospital in Scotland. There, on 17 August 1917, he met Siegfried Sassoon, who had so far published far more poetry than Owen and whose encouragement was of great value to Owen. The two poets took a keen interest in each other's poetry and in each other's problems of conscience. Sassoon helped Owen by

warning him against the 'over-lusciousness' and embarrassing senti-
mentality of his early poetry. Owen admitted his debt to Sassoon in a
letter in which he said:

> I spun round you like a satellite for a month, but I shall swing out
> soon, a dark star in the orbit where you will blaze.

He wrote a few satirical poems that were successful imitations of
Sassoon's bitter epigrams, but his most typical and inspired poetry is
quite different from Sassoon's.

Although Owen and Sassoon came very near to accepting the
principle of pacifism, Owen insisted on being sent back to the front in
September 1918. He felt that he had to return to France in order to
remain a spokesman, in his poetry, for the men in the front line.

On 4 October 1918, after most of his company had been killed, he
and a corporal captured a German machine gun and scores of prisoners;
for this feat he was awarded the M.C. But a week before the Armistice,
on 4 November 1918, he was killed when trying to construct a make-
shift bridge so as to lead his company over the Sambre Canal in the
face of heavy machine-gun fire.

As a poet his major technical innovation was the use of para-
rhymes, such as when he rhymes 'leaves' with 'lives', or 'killed' with
'cold'. Instead of changing the last consonant of the rhyming syllable,
Owen changes the vowel. This sort of half-rhyme occurs in popular
phrases such as 'riff-raff'. When Owen uses this type of rhyme the
half-rhymes shock us and suggest a mood of darkness, frustration and
melancholy which is in keeping with the tragic gloom of his themes.

One of his technical problems was how to make appropriate use of
the sensuous romantic language that he had copied from Keats, whose
poetry he admired so intensely. In some of his most moving war poems
he uses it effectively for contrast.

PALMER, EDWARD VANCE (p. 119)

Born at Bundaberg, Queensland, in 1885. As a young man he tried
many different jobs—including clerk, journalist, freelance writer and
book-keeper—and travelled in Europe, America and Asia. During the
First World War he served in France with the Australian Army.
Afterwards he returned to live near Melbourne and became one of
Australia's leading writers. He is well known for both the wide variety
and the high quality of his poems, plays, short stories and novels. Died
in 1959.

PLOWMAN, MAX (pp. 58–9)

Born at Tottenham in 1883. He held a commission in the West York-
shire Regiment and fought on the Somme. He eventually wrote a
bitter prose account of his war experiences in A *Subaltern on the
Somme*. He became a pacifist and was Secretary of the Peace Pledge
Union 1937–8. He was editor of the quarterly magazine *The Adelphi*
from 1938 to 1941, the year of his death.

READ, SIR HERBERT (pp. 72–4, 123–4)

Born at Kirbymoorside, in the remote eastern hills of the North Riding
of Yorkshire, in 1893. When his father, a farmer, died, he went to a
boarding school in Halifax and then earned his living for some years
as a bank clerk in Leeds. He later became a student of law at Leeds
University and joined the Yorkshire Regiment, the Green Howards,
from the university O.T.C. He fought in France for three years with
this regiment and won the M.C. and the D.S.O. He wrote many
important books on prose style, art appreciation and other cultural
topics. As a poet he was a consistent admirer of the Imagists,
who revolted against the unreal poetic language of the Georgians, and
made use of precise, vital images. He wrote most of his poetry in the
1930s by which time the Imagists' creed had achieved wide acceptance.
Died in 1968.

RHYS, ERNEST PERCIVAL (p. 89)

Born in 1859, he qualified as a mining engineer in 1886. He went to
London to write, and earned money as a reviewer, and was a member
of Rhymers' Club (which included Yeats, Arthur Symons and Ernest
Dowson). He contributed to the club's two publications, in 1892 and
1894. He is best known as the editor of the *Everyman Library*. Died
in 1946.

RICKWORD, EDGELL (p. 57)

Born in 1898 at Colchester. He fought on the Western Front and
published many war poems in periodicals. Most of them were written
in the 1920s.

ROSENBERG, ISAAC (pp. 68–71)

Born in 1890 in Bristol of a poor Jewish family. His father was
Lithuanian and his mother Latvian. The family moved to the East End

of London and when he left the Stepney Board School at 14 he was apprenticed to a firm of engravers in Fleet Street. Temporarily his luck changed, and three rich Jewish ladies paid for him to be trained at the Slade School as a painter. He won prizes for painting and began to write poetry. In June 1914 he moved to Cape Town in an attempt to defeat an incipient attack of tuberculosis, but he returned in May 1915 and enlisted with the Suffolk Regiment, transferring later to the King's Own Royal Lancaster Regiment. He may have suffered more during the war than any other poet; as a weak, absent-minded, artistic Jew he was bullied by both his officers and his fellow soldiers; unlike most of the poets he never enjoyed the occasional comforts of life as an officer; he hated the physical violence and the ugliness of war; he served for twenty months in the front line with only two brief periods of rest from it. His poetry, like Owen's, remained almost unknown and almost unpublished during his lifetime, though he corresponded with Marsh, Abercrombie and Binyon, who encouraged him to go on writing. He was killed on the Somme on 1 April 1918, during the big German advance.

SASSOON, SIEGFRIED (pp. 27, 33, 43, 60–1, 80–3, 103–7, 118, 122)

Born at Matfield, Kent, in 1886, a member of a rich Jewish family. In the 1890s his aunt Rachel found time to edit *The Observer* and *The Sunday Times* simultaneously. For several years he enjoyed country life as a rich young man who was keen on hunting and cricket. He later wrote a fascinating account of these years in his semi-autobiographical book *Memoirs of a Fox-Hunting Man*. This ambivalent book expresses the self-centred happiness of fox-hunting enthusiasts, but it was written much later, by a man whose new political ideas had made him sympathize with the miners and other underprivileged classes, so he was careful to include in his picture of the fox-hunting classes all the facts that a sterner critic of them would have stressed. As an autobiography his book is misleading in one important aspect; for the real Siegfried Sassoon, unlike the fictitious George Sherston, was resolved to be a poet, and wrote pleasant, uninspired verse about the country in conventional metres and language. As a fashionable young poet he was encouraged by Marsh and introduced to Brooke.

Sassoon enlisted in the Sussex Yeomanry on 3 August 1914 but he broke his arm when falling from his horse; consequently he did not go to the front till November 1915 and until then his poetry showed much the same attitude to war as Brooke's did. Early in 1916 he was fighting on the Western Front with the Royal Welch Fusiliers. He showed remarkable and rather eccentric courage. His heroic episodes in bringing back wounded from no man's land and in capturing a trench full of Germans single-handed won him the M.C.; these episodes were described by Robert Graves, an officer in the same regiment, in *Good-bye to All That.*

In July 1916 he was invalided home; on leave he became a virtual pacifist and met Liberal M.P.s who were trying to arrange a compromise peace. He had lost faith in the ethical cause for which the Allies were fighting, and in the strategy and tactics used by Allied generals on the Western Front. He was therefore the first poet to publish poetry that was openly critical of the Allies' motives and methods in waging the war. By the spring of 1917 he was back in the front line at the Battle of Arras and was wounded in the neck. Invalided home again he adopted more dramatic methods of showing his opposition to the war. Graves persuaded Sassoon to appear before an army medical board, which sent him to a hospital for neurasthenics at Craiglockart in Scotland, where he was treated by a well-known psychiatrist, Dr W. H. R. Rivers, and where he encouraged a fellow-patient, Wilfred Owen, in writing poetry.

In the 1920s he continued to show his distrust of England's ruling classes in several ways. He became the first literary editor of the new Socialist newspaper, the *Daily Herald*, and his prose books such as *Memoirs of an Infantry Officer* implied considerable criticism of the class system. For the rest of his life he continued to write competent verse, especially on rural topics. Indeed, both he and Blunden began and ended as pleasant writers of minor poetry about the countryside. Died in 1967.

SEEGER, ALAN (pp. 30–2)

Born in 1888 in New York. After living a bohemian life in Paris and researching in the British Museum library, he enlisted in the French Foreign Legion as one of a group of forty Americans. Seeger and most of the others were killed on the Somme on 4 July 1916, when six German machine-guns enfiladed them. Their sensational death was made headline news in American newspapers.

SERVICE, ROBERT WILLIAM (pp. 119–20)

Born in 1874 in Preston. He went to Canada in 1894 and joined the Canadian Bank of Commerce and spent eight years in the Yukon.

While there he wrote popular poems and novels. He was war correspondent to the *Toronto Star* during the Balkan war of 1912–13 and at the beginning of the First World War; but he later spent two years as a stretcher-bearer and ambulance driver on the Western Front. He was famous as a writer of popular verse.

SITWELL, SIR OSBERT (pp. 108–10)

Born in 1892 in London. Like his brother and sister, Sacheverell and Edith, he has been well known for most of a long life both as a poet and as a writer of very varied prose works.

He entered the Sherwood Rangers as a regular officer, but in 1912 he transferred to the Grenadier Guards, with whom he fought at Loos and throughout the war. In the end he reacted against his war experiences and his upper-class upbringing, writing satirical poetry and novels. Later he wrote very interesting memoirs about his family and achieved considerable success as a writer of short stories. In *Who's Who* he flippantly describes his recreations as 'listening to the sound of his own voice, preferably on gramophone records, and not answering letters'.

SORLEY, CHARLES HAMILTON (pp. 33, 40)

Born in Aberdeen in 1895. His father was Professor of Philosophy at Cambridge and his cousin was to have a long political career as the Conservative statesman, Lord Butler. He enlisted in the Suffolk Regiment in August 1914; he had been studying in Germany after leaving school, but managed to get out of Germany on 2 August. He was only twenty when he was killed in action on 13 October 1915 during the Battle of Loos; he was shot in the head by a sniper as he led his company in an attack. The realism of his poetry, and the intellectual independence that is revealed in his letters, have led critics to speculate as to whether he was—next to Owen—the most promising of the poets killed in the war. He saw that poetry needed to make a new start; and so he applauded the rather different attempts of Hardy and Masefield to write less romantic poetry. But he was very critical of Brooke's war sonnets and even of Hardy's poem 'Men Who March Away'; he found them equally self-righteous.

His *Marlborough and Other Poems* (1916) ran quickly into six editions and has been reprinted several times since 1918. His 'Song of the Ungirt Runners', not a war poem, has remained popular with anthologists.

THOMAS, EDWARD (pp. 23, 87)

Born in 1878 in London (of Welsh parents). Among the friends who encouraged him to write poetry were Robert Frost (the American poet, then living in England), Lascelles Abercrombie and Rupert Brooke. He wrote only a few war poems, and is best known for his poems about the Gloucestershire countryside, which are more realistic and more conversational than that of the Georgians. He was killed in action at Arras on 9 April 1917.

VERNÈDE, R. E. (p. 44)

Born in London in 1875. He wrote several novels before the war, and was a friend of G. K. Chesterton, with whom he went to school. Although he was 39 when the war broke out, he insisted on volunteering and fought in France with the 3rd Rifle Brigade. He was wounded on the Somme in 1916 but refused a job at the War Office and asked to be sent back to France. He was killed in action on 9 April 1917, the same day on which Edward Thomas died, when he was leading an attack on Havrincourt Wood. G. K. Chesterton said of him,

No man could look more lazy and no man was more active.

Index of First Lines